National Council of Teachers of English

Research Report No. 1

The Language of Elementary School Children

THE LANGUAGE OF ELEMENTARY SCHOOL CHILDREN

A Study of the Use and Control of Language
and the Relations among
Speaking, Reading, Writing, and Listening

by
WALTER LOBAN

NCTE Research Report No. 1

NATIONAL COUNCIL OF TEACHERS OF ENGLISH
508 South Sixth Street, Champaign, Illinois

NATIONAL COUNCIL OF TEACHERS OF ENGLISH

Committee on Publications

James R. Squire, NCTE Executive Secretary, *Chairman*
Jarvis E. Bush, Wisconsin State College, Oshkosh
Autrey Nell Wiley, Texas Woman's University
Miriam E. Wilt, Temple University
Enid M. Olson, NCTE Director of Publications

Consulting Readers of This Manuscript

Margaret J. Early, Syracuse University, and Patrick J. Groff, San Diego State College, read the manuscript for the Committee on Research, which is sponsoring it. Additional suggestions were made by W. Nelson Francis, Brown University, and Harold B. Allen, University of Minnesota.

National Council of Teachers of English

Research Report No. 1

is the first of a new series of publications that will make more easily available to the profession recent research studies of significance to the teaching of English. It is the aim of this series to present sufficiently detailed descriptions of research design and procedures, and sufficiently explicit findings, to enable readers to study the bases for conclusions drawn by the investigator.

Less detailed than the original study, each Research Report is more comprehensive than the limited summary which may appear in reviews and syntheses. Although scholars will wish to obtain the original study in many cases, most readers will find the Research Report the most satisfactory introduction to a particular piece of research. Thus this series fills a need not now served by other NCTE publications, or by pamphlets like the NEA research series for classroom teachers, or the summaries of research in the *Review of Educational Research*, the *Encyclopedia of Educational Research*, and the bulletins of the National Conference on Research in English.

Current vigorous interest in the research bases for teaching English is evident in the number of studies recently completed or in progress under federal and private grants. *Project English*, sponsored by the U. S. Office of Education, will increase this number. Coming at a time when research in the field of English is rapidly expanding, the NCTE Research Reports provide one more outlet for an accumulating body of information that deserves the careful attention of the profession.

To launch this series, the NCTE Committee on Research asked Professor Walter Loban to report his findings to date in a longitudinal study of the language of school children. Professor Loban's response to this request is Research Report No. 1, *The Language of Elementary School Children*. An auspicious beginning for a new series, this first report sets high standards in form and content. It is a model of readable writing, proving that a complex study can be described in plain language.

v

Appropriately, this first report exemplifies several of the functions of research. One of its contributions, for example, is the refinement of a procedure for analyzing language development. The research design is one that can be replicated so that the present findings can be supported, or challenged.

Another important function of research is to reveal new insights. This study identifies two new criteria for distinguishing stages of growth in language: mazes and evidence of tentative thinking.

Still another function of research is to verify hunches, to support or reject prior guesses, to bring new evidence to bear on old questions. This study presents data on such questions as the size of children's vocabulary, the use and control of sentence patterns, and the interrelations of oral language and competence in writing, reading, and listening.

Cautious interpretation of data is a hallmark of wisdom in writing—and reading—research reports. The blind leap from basic data to classroom applications should be avoided. Thus Professor Loban warns that "any emphasis on structure at the expense of awareness of successful communication could be a dangerous result" of careless interpretation of his data.

A major function of research is to generate new hunches, to identify new questions for study. In Professor Loban's words, "Research of this kind . . . is like the preliminary explorations of a vast continent." Research Report No. 1 is an invitation to explore, with scientific detachment, the language development of American students.

MARGARET EARLY, *Chairman*
Committee on Research

ACKNOWLEDGEMENTS

The work on this study has been made possible by the sustained efforts of a number of workers. From the beginning, Mrs. Elaine Olsen assisted in all phases of the study. She was joined shortly thereafter by Mrs. Vera Reiche, who is still with the study. Miss Virginia Mini, during her years as coordinator, gave the study an orderliness it had previously lacked. Mrs. Marilyn Williams, research analyst, has contributed perceptively to every aspect of the work, and Mrs. Gertrude Funkhauser has handled all the correspondence and the relationships with the United States Office of Education. Dr. Evelyn Fix, Department of Statistics, University of California at Berkeley, guided the original planning of the design, and the statistical analyses have been carried out with integrity by Mrs. Dorothy Seiden and Mr. Arthur Williams. As consultants Mrs. Luella B. Cook, Dr. James Sledd, and Mr. John Dennis made contributions requiring their special competence in research design and structural linguistics.

A conference with Dr. Ruth Strickland, Professor of Education, Indiana University, was made possible by the assistance of the Cooperative Research Program of the United States Office of Education. At this conference, held in Bloomington, Indiana, the following linguists provided special assistance: John Carroll, Harvard University; W. Nelson Francis, now of Brown University; Fred Householder, Indiana University; David Reed, University of California at Berkeley; Harold Whitehall, Indiana University.

Fortunately the writer had an understanding administrative superior, William A. Brownell, Dean of the School of Education, University of California, Berkeley. Dean Brownell protected the writer from anxieties that can arise when a research plan does not yield rapid results or numerous publications. Dean Brownell also read and criticized with great care the early designs and rough drafts, bringing to bear upon them an impressive integrity and knowledge.

To these helpers and to others who have worked part time upon occasion, the director of the research wishes to acknowledge his sincere appreciation. Longitudinal research is expensive in time, energy, and money, and indeed this has been a "cooperative project" on more levels than that between the United States Office of Education and the University of California.

WALTER LOBAN
University of California, Berkeley

The research reported herein was supported through the Cooperative Research Program of the Office of Education, United States Department of Health, Education, and Welfare. The original study, summarized in the present research report, is entitled *Language Ability in the Middle Grades of the Elementary School*, a report to the United States Department of Health, Education, and Welfare by Walter Loban, March 1, 1961. This report is available at 100 depositories throughout the nation.

TABLE OF CONTENTS

Chapter One:

Chapter Three:

TABLE OF CONTENTS—Continued

TABLES

FIGURES

Chapter One

RESEARCH DESIGN AND PROCEDURES

PURPOSES OF THE INVESTIGATION

The research reported in this monograph is a study of language used by children in the kindergarten and first six years of elementary school. It is concerned with their use and control of language, their effectiveness in communication, and with the relations among their oral, written, listening, and reading uses of language. It is one part of a longer study covering the same subjects throughout the elementary and secondary school years.

The study is also concerned with developing fundamental methods of analysis to aid the scientific study of children's language and to locate significant features of language worthy of further study.

The major questions forming the purposes and dimensions of this longitudinal research were these:

. . . Just as in physical development, are there predictable stages of growth in language?

. . . Can definite sequences in language development be identified?

. . . How do children vary in ability with language and gain proficiency in using it?

DESIGN OF THE RESEARCH, A BRIEF OVERVIEW

This research is based on a developmental design with the hypotheses and methods subject to modification during the course of a continuing study. The subjects were in 1952 a representative group of 338 kindergarten children. At regular intervals over a period of eleven years, comparable samples of their language have been collected.[1] From this evidence significant features worthy of description and analysis have been identified and studied.

---

[1]The total longitudinal study has been planned for a period to include the subjects' school years from kindergarten through grade twelve. This monograph reports only the first seven years—the elementary years—of this total time period, 1952-1965.

1

The samples of language—speech, writing, reading—have been drawn once a year from controlled situations identical for all subjects. Data on listening were collected later in the study. In order that other research workers might use the same procedures for purposes of further application, verification, or refutation, the data have also been collected and analyzed by methods allowing for repetition. Wherever applicable and appropriate, standard procedures of quantitative and statistical description have been used. New methods have been carefully described. Thus it is possible to present the status of the subjects' language ability at equally spaced periods of time. Whether one is interested in normative data for the group or in changes occurring to individuals, the data will provide answers.

In addition to the larger representative group of subjects, two special subgroups have been selected from the total sample. These two subgroups consist of subjects representing extreme deviations from the mean of the total sample.[2] In the first special subgroup are those ranking extremely high in language proficiency; in the second subgroup are those extremely low in language ability. For these two special groups more extensive data have been gathered and analyzed.[3]

THE SAMPLE

The 338 subjects used in this study were chosen to represent a stratified sample of a larger universe of children. Eleven kindergarten classes were matched with family backgrounds typical of the city of Oakland, California. Thus subjects included a range of family status from definitely poor economic circumstances in the industrial areas down by the Bay through the middle class areas up to the more favored socioeconomic circumstances of the hill-top districts. The

---

[2]The basis of selection was the vocabulary test given in the kindergarten year and the average of four or more years of teachers' ratings of the subjects' language ability. These two scores were given equal weight in determining the subgroups, and all subjects two or more standard deviations from the mean were selected to comprise the high and low subgroups. From the fourth grade and thereafter, these two criteria were used in lieu of any better or established standards of general language proficiency. By means of these two criteria as temporary means of selecting subgroups, the experimenter proposes to locate empirically more refined evidence of language proficiency. Whenever one of the subjects high or low in the study moved from the area, the next subject in line for the group was used as a replacement.

[3]The N in the two groups will sometimes vary because occasionally a score for some subject will not be available or usable for some specific reason. Usually there are from 24 to 30 subjects in any one subgroup.

evidence on socioeconomic status for the subjects in this research places the median slightly below middle class.[4]

However, stratification was not tied to one particular variable such as socioeconomic status. The choice of subjects also included representativeness on the bases of sex, racial background, and spread of intellectual ability. Care was taken to avoid any unique or unusual factor of selection. In other words, these four general stratification variables were used, together with proportional allocation. The characteristics used for defining the strata were related to the subject under investigation, inasmuch as other studies of children's language have identified socioeconomic status, sex, race, and intelligence as factors influencing language proficiency.

THE DATA COLLECTED

In the present study evidence concerning the 338 subjects' use, development, and control of language was needed for each individual. Plans were carried out to collect data concerning (a) their vocabulary, (b) their use of oral and written language, (c) their proficiency in reading and listening, (d) teachers' judgments of their skill with language, and (e) background information on their health and homes. These data were collected over a period of seven years, from kindergarten through grade six. (In the larger study, the collection continues until 1964-1965.)

Each subject was interviewed individually and his spoken responses recorded annually on a recording device, the Audograph. The Audograph reproduces sound on a plastic flexible disc and preserves a reliable reproduction of the subject's voice.[5] Each interview followed a standardized form and, in cases where an extra question was asked, the purpose was solely to encourage a flow of language already on its way. At the beginning of the interview, the examiner encouraged the child to become talkative by asking him questions about playmates, games, television, illness, and wishes. Next the child was

---

[4]For these subjects the median score is V, one step below the median of the Minnesota Occupational Scale. A more complete discussion of the subjects' socioeconomic classification and of the Minnesota Occupational Scale will be found on pages 26-27 of this monograph.

[5]Audographs do not reproduce the quality of voice with as much fidelity as do tape recorders, but the quality is certainly not poor. Beginning with the first grade, tape recordings as well as Audograph records were made for selected children whose linguistic behavior in the kindergarten year had proved to be particularly interesting or exceptional.

shown, for the remainder of the interview, a series of six pictures, the same pictures being used for all subjects. The pictures were chosen for their interest, their success in preliminary trials, or their value in previous research. The subjects were asked to discuss what they saw in each picture and what they thought about each picture. The recorded Audograph interviews were then transcribed into typewritten form according to a careful set of directions. These transcripts of the child's oral language constitute some of the most important data collected in the study.

Additional data include measures of the subject's intelligence and evidence of achievement in vocabulary, use of relational words (such as *however, consequently*), and achievement in reading, writing, and listening. In addition, for each school year, the teachers rated the subjects on selected language factors and kept accurate records of school attendance. Background information on homes, parental occupations, health, siblings, and date of birth complete the data.

TECHNIQUES

In the search for answers, many different kinds of method and analysis have been used in this research. These techniques have been classified into four groups:

. . . new methods of analysis originated for the purposes of this investigation

. . . methods of analysis derived from the research of other workers

. . . standardized tests

. . . ratings and indices for such factors as socioeconomic status, school attendance, and writing ability.

The techniques in each of these groups will be described in the paragraphs which follow.

New Methods of Analysis

1. *Segmenting the subjects' oral language.*

In this research, devising an objective method for segmenting the flow of oral language was a critical problem. Certain familiar systems of dividing language into segments proved to be inadequate. Words alone, for instance, offer a crude basis for numerical count but show nothing about relations among ideas. Traditional grammatical divisions, such as sentences, also blur important distinctions and often do not correspond to the actuality of oral language where utterances may be only phrases or single words. The system of segmentation finally chosen was one which combined several approaches. First the subjects' speech was segmented by oral intonation patterns and then, within such intonation segments, syntactic units (each independent predication) were identified.[6]

   . . . The first of these—intonation pattern—is dependent upon the patterns of sound made by the human voice; it is judged by the contours of inflection, stress, and pause in the subjects' voices. Because the segmentation is made in accordance with the sound-system of English, this first and more comprehensive segment will be called a *phonological unit.*

   . . . The second unit, always a subdivision of the larger phonological unit, will be called a *communication unit* because it can be identified by the semantic meaning which is being communicated.

   . . . Beyond these two kinds of segmentation, a third element still remained to be accounted for, an exceptionally interesting and frequent occurrence that could best be described as a tangle of language which did not make semantic sense and was impossible to classify phonologically or semantically. These language tangles have, therefore, been segmented separately and have been labeled *mazes.* Each of these three segments will now be described more fully and illustrated by examples.

---

[6]This choice of segmentation is the outcome of a conference sponsored by the U.S. Department of Health, Education, and Welfare and held at Bloomington, Indiana, in October of 1959. The linguistic consultants at this conference were John Carroll, W. Nelson Francis, Fred Householder, David Reed, and Harold Whitehall. The conference established a conformity of method for the research being reported in this monograph and for that of Ruth Strickland, whose similar research into the language of children may now be consulted in *The Language of Elementary School Children: Its Relationship to the Language of Reading Textbooks and the Quality of Reading of Selected Children.* Bulletin of the School of Education, Indiana University, 38: 4 (July, 1962). Bloomington: Indiana University, 1962.

The phonological unit.—An example will help to make clear what the phonological unit is in this study. One child in the study said the following words:

> I'm going to get a boy| 'cause he hit me.# I'm going to beat him up and kick him in his nose|| and I'm going to get the girl, too.#

The silence pauses of the subject's speech, in association with his use of pitch, show two double-cross junctures (#). The double-cross is a mark to show a pause or juncture in speech which is a clear-cut termination to an utterance. It is usually marked by a definite pause preceded by a diminishing of force and a drop in the pitch of the voice (or a rise in pitch for queries). The other two marks—double-bar juncture (||) and single-bar juncture (|)—represent silence pauses of less finality. In this example, the speaker used two definite phonological units, units characterized by definite pauses following a definite drop in pitch.[7] The phonological unit, then, is an utterance occurring between the silences represented by double-cross junctures. If the example given in this passage seems to show phonological units to be identical with traditional grammatical "sentences," the reader may be assured that the subjects in this study often did not let their voices drop and pause at the end of every traditional sentence. Moreover, the subjects sometimes answered questions in phonological units that were, grammatically, subordinate clauses.

The communication unit.—The communication unit has been defined by Watts as a group of words which cannot be further divided without the loss of their essential meaning.[8] For instance, "I know a boy with red hair" is a unit of communication. If "with red hair" is omitted, the essential meaning of that particular unit of communication has been changed. "I know a boy" does not mean the same thing as "I know a boy with red hair." In all cases, the words comprising a communication unit are examples of grammatical independent predication or they are answers to questions which lack only the repetition of the question elements to satisfy the criterion of independent

---

[7]For a more complete discussion of these terms, see W. Nelson Francis, *The Structure of American English* (New York: Ronald Press, 1958), p. 157, and Archibald A. Hill, *Introduction to Linguistic Structures* (New York: Harcourt, Brace & World, 1958), pp. 13-30.

[8]This is what A. F. Watts calls "the natural linguistic unit." See A. F. Watts, *The Language and Mental Development of Children* (Boston: D. C. Heath & Company, 1948), pp. 65-66.

predication. On the other hand, "Yes" can be admitted as a unit of communication when it is an answer to a question such as "Have you ever been sick?" Thus, these units prove to be not exclusively semantic; they are also syntactic, being composed of independent predications; they can be identified by their form as well as by their meaning. Since "essential meaning" might be difficult to define scientifically, the formal definition of an independent clause between two silences becomes more defensible than the semantic (or meaning) definition.

The following examples illustrate quickly the method of tallying these communication units of language. A slant line (/) marks the completion of each communication unit. (The # marks the completion of a phonological unit.)

Examples of Communication Units

Transcription of Subject's Actual Language	Communication Units	No. of Words in Each Communication Unit
I'm going to get a boy 'cause he hit me.#/ I'm going to beat him up an' kick him in his nose‖ / and I'm going to get the girl, too.#/	3	11 13 9

Note that the first communication unit could not be divided after "boy" without the disappearance of (1) its essential meaning and (2) a subordinate clause that is part of the independent predication. Note in the last two communication units that a compound predicate with the same subject is classified as one unit, but a compound *sentence* (which *can* be divided without essential loss of meanings) becomes two communication units. This distinction is of importance to this study and should be noted carefully by the reader. In actuality, the communication unit in this research proves to be the grammatical independent clause with any of its modifiers. No communication unit includes more than one such clause. Thus this second kind of segmentation can actually be achieved structurally, but the use of meaning does reinforce the method of segmentation adopted for this research. Some linguists have been critical of any use of "communication" or meaning, urging a rigorous use of structure alone. The writer, however, has seen no problem in using meaning as a double check on the structural methodology which is actually being used. By so doing, some mistakes have been located, no dilemmas have arisen, and the research has retained a closer alliance with the ultimate purpose of language.

The language maze.—One cannot listen to these recordings or read the transcripts without noting how frequently the subjects, when they attempt to express themselves, become confused or tangled in words. This confusion occurs not only in interview situations but also in the daily talk of the children, in the classroom when they share experiences, and on the playground of the school. The language behavior in question is not a matter of words tumbling over one another but rather a case of many hesitations, false starts, and meaningless repetitions. In this research these language tangles have been labeled *mazes*. The linguistic troubles of the subjects resemble very much the physical behavior of a person looking for a way out of an actual spatial maze. He thrashes about in one direction or another until, finally, he either abandons his goal or locates a path leading where he wishes to go. Sometimes he stumbles upon a way out; sometimes he has presence of mind enough to pause and reason a way out.

These *mazes* are a series of words or initial parts of words which do not add up, either to meaningful communication or to structural units of communication as defined in this research. They are unattached fragments or a series of unattached fragments which do not constitute a communication unit and are not necessary to the communication unit.

Sometimes the mazes are very long, consisting of from ten to twenty or more words or fragments of words. Sometimes the subjects persevere with the ideas they are trying to formulate and, at the end of the maze, do achieve a unit of communication. Other times the subjects abandon the ideas they are trying to express, perhaps finding the problem too difficult or too tiring to express, or not worth the effort. It is entirely possible that in another situation, where the motivation was much greater, the same idea represented in the maze might find its way to a clear expression of meaning. The energy level or the health of the subject may also be decisive factors in the child's success or failure in converting an idea into a genuine unit of communication.

Examples of Mazes

(Mazes are in brackets. The number of words in the maze is circled.)[9]

Transcription of Subject's Actual Language	Communication Units	No. of Words in Comm. Units
1. (Short maze at the beginning of a communication unit and integrally related to that communication unit.) ["I'm goin'] . . . I'm goin' to build a flying saucer/ but I can't think how yet."#	2	③- 8 7
2. (Short maze in the middle of a communication unit and integrally related to that communication unit.) "When I was fixin' ready to go home, my mother called me up in the house/ an' [an' an' have to] I have to get my hair combed."#	2	16 1 -④- 7
3. (Long maze not immediately related to a communication unit. The child apparently drops the whole project as being too complicated for his powers.) "I saw a hunter program last Sunday/ [an' he, an' snow time he had to have lot uh, wah-h when he, uh, not too many dogs, he] . . . and that's all I think of that picture."#	2	7 ⑱ 9

Such mazes are not counted as communication units. The procedure has been to count the words in them, however, and then circle this count. The reader will note that when a maze is removed from a communication unit, the remaining material *always* constitutes a straightforward, acceptable communication unit. Furthermore, just as the communication units fall within phonological units, so too do the mazes fall within phonological units.

These three methods of analysis ([1] the phonological unit, [2] the communication unit, and [3] the maze) were applied to the transcripts of the subjects and have become the basis for what is called in

---

[9]In the actual transcript, the analyst always brackets and encircles mazes with red pencil.

this research the First Level of Analysis. The following rules summarize the method of segmentation used in this research:

1) Every utterance must contain at least one communication unit. Hence an utterance which is not an independent clause but which is preceded and followed by (terminal) silence on the part of the child is arbitrarily defined as a communication unit.

2) The material in a stretch between terminal silence and terminal silence contains at least as many communication units as it contains independent clauses. Every independent clause is a communication unit; no communication unit contains more than one independent clause.

3) In a stretch between terminal silences, material which precedes, separates, or follows independent clauses constitutes either mazes or further communication units. Every stretch of this material which constitutes an elliptical independent clause (such that it could be expanded into an independent clause by the simple repetition of words from the context) is a communication unit.

4) A word like *yes* or *no* is a separate communication unit when it could be replaced by an independent clause. It is not a separate unit when it could not be replaced by an independent clause but merely introduces such a clause.

First Level of Analysis.—The communication units, constituting either phonological units or parts of phonological units, come close to being what are traditionally known as sentences. But to ignore the phonological method of segmentation would mean to disregard important clues. Thus, to the syntactic and meaning approaches to language, we have joined the phonological. The result proves to be one which makes *maximum use both of structure and of meaning*. Although communication units are not inevitably segmented by double-cross junctures, they are usually so marked. In instances where they are not, either a double-bar or a single-bar juncture does occur *without exception*. Thus assured of genuine segmentation, the research worker can next ask what to do with the segments.

In this research, the decision was to classify the communication units according to a system of basic structural patterns such as the following:

. . .   Subject—Verb   George eats.
. . .   Subject—Verb—Object   George eats onions.

. . . Subject–Linking Verb–Predicate Nominative	Onions are roots.
. . . Subject–Linking Verb–Predicate Adjective	Onions are good.
. . . Subject–Verb–Inner Object–Object	George gave John an onion.

Nine patterns, representing basic structures of the English sentence, were used. This First Level of Analysis, then, shows the frequency and variety of structural patterns used by the subjects. It will show whether or not children know these patterns before they come to school, merely elaborating them thereafter, or whether they learn to use some of these patterns after they have entered school. It will show whether some children use certain patterns more often than others. It will show whether or not the same patterns of structure are used for writing as for speaking, and it could be used to show whether or not the patterns occurring in children's readers correspond to the patterns children use in their speech.

SYMBOLS USED IN ANALYSIS OF COMMUNICATION UNITS

To simplify the technique of analysis on this First Level, the following symbols were used:[10]

	2						Ƶ								
1	②	3	4	5	6	M	△Z	X	U	+	╪	T	O	W	?

1 = subject
This includes both the head (central word) and its modifiers (articles, appositives, restrictive and nonrestrictive phrases and clauses).

1

Example: [The fat robin with the sharp bill] was flying swiftly.

[10]This formula was devised for the research of both Strickland (see footnote 6 on page 5) and Loban at the Bloomington conference previously mentioned. The use of numbers is solely a convenience, saving time in tallying and coding. Otherwise, a system such as N, V, LV might be just as useful.

2   and ② = verbs used as predicates
This includes the head (the main verb) plus auxiliary verbs
and modifiers.

$$2$$

Example: The fat robin │was flying swiftly.│

2 represents transitive and intransitive verbs.

$$2$$

Examples: The robin │eats.│

$$2$$

The robin │eats│ worms.

② represents linking verbs.

$$②$$

Examples: The bird │is│ a robin.

$$②$$

The bird │is│ red.

$$②$$

The music │sounded│ loud.

3 = the inner complement (indirect object)

$$3$$

Example: She gave │the boy│ some bread.

4 = the transitive verb complement (direct object)

$$4$$

Example: The machine crushed │the rock.│

5 = the linking verb complement (adjectival, nominal, or other
element used as subjective complement)

$$5$$

Examples: The bird is a │robin.│

$$5$$

The bird is │red.│

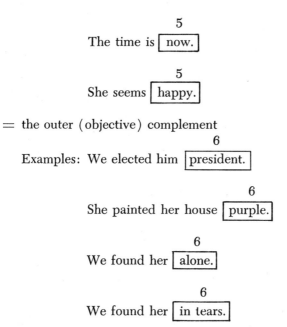

The time is $\boxed{\overset{5}{\text{now.}}}$

She seems $\boxed{\overset{5}{\text{happy.}}}$

6 = the outer (objective) complement

Examples: We elected him $\boxed{\overset{6}{\text{president.}}}$

She painted her house $\boxed{\overset{6}{\text{purple.}}}$

We found her $\boxed{\overset{6}{\text{alone.}}}$

We found her $\boxed{\overset{6}{\text{in tears.}}}$

M = the movable parts of a sentence (words, phrases, or clauses with no fixed position. However, the degree of "movability" varies. Some elements prove to be more movable than others.)

Examples: Boys $\boxed{\overset{M}{\text{usually}}}$ like dogs better than cats.

$\boxed{\overset{M}{\text{The rain having stopped,}}}$ they went home.

Ƶ = a maze
    Example: [. . . an' he, an' snow time he had to have lot uh, wah-h when he, uh, not too many dogs, he . . .]

⟁ = a false start, a shift in expression, but not the confusion of a maze

Example: I was going to buy $\boxed{\overset{⟁}{\text{three little . . . no,}}}$ four big

bars.

X = words of little meaning value used as primers or launchers (well, see, you know, let's see, yeah) or as fillers (or something, and so forth)

U = short utterance, a word or group carrying meaning, with a falling intonation (Yes, O.K., I think so.)

+ = a sentence connector (and, but, so, and so)

$\neq$ = subordinators, subordinators used as connectors (until, since, if, although, because, etc.)

T = topic followed by subject

Example: $\boxed{\overset{\text{T}}{\text{The man in the picture,}}}$ well, he is thinking about his pal.

O = ellipsis of an essential part of the sentence

W = question words (who, when, why, what, where, how)

? = unanalyzable construction (This is not a maze but a construction about which the analyst cannot be certain; these occur with extreme rarity, for almost always the combination of phonological, syntactic, and semantic evidence dispels the need for a ?.)

PATTERNS OF COMMUNICATION UNITS

Applying these symbols to the communication units then became the next step. Each communication unit, it will be remembered, is a syntactic unit verified by two methods—the fact that phonologically it is separated from the surrounding language by an intonation juncture and the fact that grammatically it is or contains an independent predication which communicates meaning. Analysis shows that *all* communication units, once any mazes have been cleared away, may be classified under the following nine patterns and one partial or incomplete unit:

Pattern	*Symbol*	*Examples*
one	1 2 or 1 ②	Mary eats. (or) Mary is home.
two	1 2 4	Mary eats strawberries.

three	1 ② 5	Strawberries are berries.
		Strawberries are good.
four	1 2 3 4	Mary threw the dog some biscuits.
five	1 2 4 6	They elected Mary president.
		They thought Susie conceited.
six	(1) ② 1	Here is Mary.
		There are four houses on Lime Street.
seven	Questions	How does he do it? Is he here?
eight	Passive forms	Strawberries were eaten by Mary.
nine	Requests, commands	Go home. (or) Let us go home.
(ten)	Partials	Any incomplete unit (This is not actually a pattern like the preceding nine patterns.)

Second Level of Analysis.—The Second Level of Analysis is a deeper analysis of the elements comprising the First Level of Analysis. The First Level provides a skeleton picture of communication units which may then be examined for patterns of structure, a matter of genuine importance in linguistic study, whereas the Second Level examines the component parts of the pattern displayed at the First Level. Do some children use more subordinate clauses than others? Which children use only single words for subjects, objects, or complements, and which ones use more complicated nominals, infinitives, clauses, and verbal phrases? From the First Level of Analysis any element in the formula—the M's (movables), the 1's (subjects), the Z's or any other element—may be chosen for more complete analysis on the Second Level. For instance, what repertoire of movables does a child produce? Does he use single words only or elaborate clusters of phrases and clauses? What does a study of his verbs reveal? The possibilities of fruitful analysis at the Second Level are numerous.

2. *Function of communication units.*

Another tool of analysis is the classification of the subjects' speech in terms of function. This method—requiring great amounts of time to carry out—was used only with the two special groups included in the design of this study—the subjects designated as high and low in language skill.

In any study of language, it is desirable to consider not only quantitative aspects such as units and mazes but also qualitative aspects such as the uses to which language is put. Other research workers have classified the functions of children's speech into various categories, categories determined by the conditions under which the samples were taken. For instance, Piaget divided the functions of children's playground speech into categories of egocentric and socialized speech.[11] Rugg and others chose classifications such as self-assertion, perceptions, and linguistic experimentation.[12] The content of communication varies so greatly with the situation in which it occurs that no universal set of function-classifications has emerged from research. Categories devised for studying the functions of language will always depend on the purposes of the investigation and the situation from which the language sample is drawn. In this present research, the subjects' transcripts were studied to determine categories actually occurring in the situation from which the subjects' language was recorded. The most useful and suitable categories proved to be seven kinds of expressions:

1) facts and unelaborated perceptions
2) interpretations
3) personal associations
4) tentative statements or suppositions
5) generalizations
6) irrelevancies
7) direct questions
8) figurative language

It is worth noting that in a different situation, the categories used here might not be fully comprehensive. The functions of language shift from situation to situation. Classification in this research was not intended as a contribution to the study of function; instead, it was part of the search for techniques which might reveal differences between subjects high and low in language ability.

3. *Classification of oral language style.*

A third method of analysis created for this research was based on style rather than content. In oral language, each individual uses a distinctive style or manner of speaking, one closely related to his

---

[11]Jean Piaget, *The Language and Thought of the Child* (New York: Harcourt, Brace, & World, 1926).
[12]H. Rugg, L. Krueger, and A. Sondergaard, "Studies in Child Personality: I. A Study of the Language of Kindergarten Children," *Journal of Educational Psychology*, 20 (1929), 1-18.

personality. People speak impulsively or deliberately, fluently or hesitantly, loquaciously or laconically. The outstanding features of spoken linguistic style have been known for centuries; thus it is possible for an analyst to describe such features and to focus upon one feature at a time in a situation where the recordings could be played and replayed as many times as necessary.

In this study, even in the kindergarten year, the subjects expressed themselves in highly varied styles of speech. Eleven outstanding features of spoken style were identified, each one being stated as follows in the form of a continuum scaled 1 to 3:

fluent	to	halting
deliberate	to	impulsive
coherent	to	incoherent, disorganized
energetic	to	listless, weak, tired
laconic	to	loquacious
expressive	to	flat, expressionless
mature	to	babyish
distinct, clearly articulated	to	blurred, indistinct, mumbled
conventional in usage	to	unconventional in usage
ready in response	to	slow in response
relaxed	to	tense, strained

Methods of Analysis Derived from Other Research

Four types of analysis applied to the data represent procedures already used by previous research workers. These four procedures are the (1) amount of subordination; (2) classification of conventional usage, syntax, and grammar; (3) classification of vocabulary according to frequency of use in the language; and (4) classification of vocabulary according to diversity. Each of these procedures is described in the paragraphs which follow.

Amount of subordination.—Both logical analysis and previous studies of language designate subordination as a more mature and difficult form of language expression than simple parallel statements connected by *and* or *but*.[13, 14, 15] Phrases and dependent clauses are ver-

---

[13]M. V. Bear, "Children's Growth in the Use of Written Language," *Elementary English Review*, 16 (1939), 312-19.

[14]F. K. Heider and G. M. Heider, "A Comparison of Sentence Structure of Deaf and Hearing Children," *Psychological Monographs*, 52: 1 (1940), 42-103.

[15]Lou LaBrant, "A Study of Certain Language Developments of Children in Grades 4-12 Inclusive," *Genetic Psychology Monographs*, 14:4 (1933), 387-394.

bal means of showing relationships; through them, speakers communicate more complex propositions than are possible with simple independent clauses. Furthermore, subordination makes possible a more coherent organization of related statements.

In this study, the incidence of subordination was tallied for the subjects who were exceptionally high or low in language ability and for a group of subjects chosen at random from the total sample. All subordinate clauses, both for speaking and for writing, were counted and classified according to order of subordination (first-order, second-order, etc.).[16]

The ability to express natural or logical relations does not, however, depend solely upon subordinate clauses. Prepositional phrases, infinitives, appositives, verbals, and other strategies of structure serve the proficient speaker or writer in expressing and compressing his thought. Therefore, the index of subordination, valuable though it has proved to be in revealing a degree of proficiency for subjects in this research, is nevertheless incomplete. A perfect index of structural complexity would encompass more than subordination.

A technique for studying such complexity is emerging from the current theoretical work of the American linguist, Noam Chomsky.[17] His transformation analysis is time-consuming, but it has been applied to the transcripts of two subjects in this research and shows great promise as a technique for studying children's language. The results show every indication of being a more complete and incisive extension of the subordination index used by LaBrant and by the present research. Future research in language will undoubtedly develop and use to advantage Chomsky's transformational analysis.

For our purposes here we will follow Chomsky in viewing our grammar as a system of devices which reinforce each other in gen-

---

[16]A subordinate clause which modifies an independent element of the communication unit is termed "first-order subordination." Subordination which modifies another subordinate element, which in turn modifies an independent element, is called "second-order subordination." Second-order subordination, as well as all subordination, has been established in research as the mark of mature mental activity and complex expression. (See LaBrant, footnote 15 on page 17.) A few subjects in the present research even use third-order subordination.

[17]Noam Chomsky, "Review of B. F. Skinner, *Verbal Behavior,*" *Language,* 35 (1959), 26-58.

————, *Syntactic Structures* ('s-Gravenhage: Mouton and Company, 1957).

————, "A Transformational Approach to Syntax," *Third Texas Conference on Problems of Linguistic Analysis in English, May 9-12, 1958,* ed. Archibald A. Hill (Austin: University of Texas Press, 1962).

erating and controlling grammatical utterances.[18] A knowledge of one's grammar will not, it must be pointed out, guarantee the consistent creation of grammatical sentences. Everyone who speaks English works from some kind of grammar, yet consciousness of the model is rare indeed, for as will be noted in this research, the child knows the structure of his language fairly well by the time he is in kindergarten. Nor does it follow that all models are equal in their power to generate accuracy.

Our grammar may be seen as existing and operating on two contiguous levels: (1) a phrase structure grammar and (2) a transformational grammar. The phrase structure grammar makes possible the simple, active *kernel statements* of our language—statements such as *John eats, John eats onions,* and *Onions are roots.* Within any kernel statement there are certain obligations and options. For example, a grammatical obligation in English is *concord* (or agreement) between subject and verb in active voice. The *s* on *eats* in *John eats onions* is an obligation. An option, on the other hand, is the use of a general or specific determiner or no determiner at all. Thus,

$$\left.\begin{array}{r}\text{A} \\ \text{The}\end{array}\right\} \text{boy eats} \left\{\begin{array}{l}\text{the} \\ \\ \text{a}\end{array}\right\} \text{onion.}$$

If the nominal phrase (or "complete subject") is singular or plural, the verbal phrase (or "complete predicate") is obliged to agree in person and number. On the other hand, the use of *a* or *the* is optional here. Inclusion or exclusion of modification constitutes another option in phrase structure grammar. However, it must be noted that the selection of certain types of modification can impose structural obligations.

We may think of the generation of an utterance in phrase structure grammar as a series of steps, governed by a small body of rules which tell us what order the steps should take and what options and obligations we have as we proceed. Such a model would look this way:

---

[18]The technique of transformational grammar is described by Noam Chomsky in his book *Syntactic Structures* ('s-Gravenhage: Mouton and Company, 1957). The following description of transformational analysis and application to the language of two subjects in this research has been prepared by John Dennis, Assistant Professor of Language Arts, San Francisco State College, San Francisco, California.

Step 1. NP   + VP
          singular   singular
Step 2. The N   V   NP
Step 3. The boy V a N
Step 4. The boy (C) eat a   strawberry
Step 5. The boy (present) eat a   strawberry
Step 6. The boy eats a   strawberry
Step 7. Pattern of communication unit: / 1 2 4 /

Key

N =	noun
V =	verb
P =	phrase
C =	concord, tense

Each step represents one possible choice from among many which are implicit in the previous step. Each choice sets up obligations as we proceed.

If we look now beyond the level of kernel structures, those simple active statements in our language such as the / 1 2 4 / communication unit just above, we observe the manipulation of those kernel structures according to options and obligations. We note a number of specific and general transformations. At this higher level, the much more complex structures of our language have been produced by a succession of transformations. Examples of such grammatical operations beyond phrase structure grammar include passive constructions, auxiliary transformations, questions, negative constructions, emphatic constructions (using *Do* and *Did* plus primary stress), and the use of generalized conjunction transformations (the use of *and* to link sentence elements of the same type). Again there is an order which must be observed. If an active, positive statement is to be transformed into a passive, negative one, the passive transformation must precede the negative one. Our earlier structure "The boy eats an onion" would be transformed through these steps:

Phrase structure: The boy eats an onion.
Transformation: An onion (past) be + en eat by the boy
  (passive)
Transformation: An onion be (past) eat + en by the boy
  (auxiliary)

Transformation: An onion not be (past) eat + en by the boy
(negative)
                    An onion was not eaten by the boy.

It could be argued that there is nothing "new" about this kind of operation. Grammarians have been writing about passive constructions and the use of negatives for a long time. The coining and the use of the term *transformation* itself does not bring enlightenment. However, one advantage of transformation theory and classification may be noted: through a model, what was previously explained in impressionistic or imprecise terms can now be made more orderly, explicit, and economical.

Difficulties with conventions in usage and grammar.—For a classification of nonstandard usage, syntax, and grammar, the investigator examined the categories established by Charters[19] and O'Rourke.[20] Modifications were necessary, for those earlier studies were based upon written language, and in this research the analysis of conventions is based on both written and spoken language. Consequently punctuation, spelling, and capitalization categories were omitted.[21] Thus the unconventional categories tallied for all subjects in the study were as follows:

   items involving the use of verbs
   items involving the use of pronouns
   items involving omission or repetition
   items involving the use of prepositions and conjunctions
   items involving the use of modifiers
   items involving the use of nouns (i.e., singular, plural, etc.)

Several of these categories required further subdivision in order to avoid blurring important distinctions. This analysis of usage, grammar, and syntax was carried out for all pupils in this study and for each year.

---

[19] W. W. Charters, "Minimum Essentials in Elementary Language and Grammar, A Second Report." *16th Yearbook of the National Society for the Study of Education*, Pt. I (Chicago: NSSE, 1917).

[20] L. J. O'Rourke, *Rebuilding the English Curriculum: A Report of a Nationwide Study of English* (Washington: The Psychological Institute, 1934).

[21] The writing of the subjects has been collected each year. Conventions in writing appear on pages 25-26. Further reports on writing will appear in future publications not yet completed.

Vocabulary measured by word frequencies.—Two measures of vocabulary power were based upon methods used in previous research. By using the count of word frequency by Thorndike and Lorge, the investigator was able to tally the subjects' words according to frequency of occurrence in the English language.[22] What percent of a speaker's words occur in the thousand most commonly used words? What percent occur in each of the subsequent thousands as presented in Thorndike's count of word frequency? How does the vocabulary of subjects in the high special group compare with that of the subjects in the low special group? Considerations of time and cost limited this count to the two special subgroups high and low in language power.

Vocabulary measured by diversity.—For this purpose the research uses the type-token ratio, the number of different words used in relation to the total number of words. Although the type-token ratio has sometimes been criticized, it can disclose important distinctions *when the size of language samples is kept uniform.* The type-token ratio (TTR) is the ratio of the number of different words (types) to the total number of words (tokens) in a sample of language. Johnson[23] and Chotlos[24] have used this ratio as a measure of verbal diversification, showing that a writer or speaker who uses a large vocabulary has a more diversified style than one who uses a small vocabulary.

One difficulty with the TTR is that it necessarily becomes smaller as the size of the language sample becomes larger. For instance, in the present research, the TTR could have discriminated against subjects who used the most language because as the length of a sample increases, the possibility that words will be repeated becomes greater than the likelihood that new words will occur. In order to control this factor, the investigator divided all transcripts of the subjects' oral language into segments of 100 words and in each segment counted only the new words that had not appeared before in any preceding segment. From these counts curves were con-

[22]E. L. Thorndike and I. Lorge, *The Teacher's Word Book of 30,000 Words* (New York: Teachers College, Columbia University, Bureau of Publications, 1944).

[23]Wendell Johnson, "Studies in Language Behavior: I. A Program of Research," *Psychological Monographs,* 56:2 (1944).

[24]J. W. Chotlos, "Studies in Language Behavior: IV. A Statistical and Comparative Analysis of Individual Written Language Samples," *Psychological Monographs,* 56 (1944), 75-111.

structed, plotting the number of new words per segment. These curves show directly the rate at which members of both special subgroups introduced new words into the language samples.

Tests

Three tests were administered to the subjects—a vocabulary test used solely in this study; the Kuhlmann-Anderson Intelligence Test; and a test of ability to use subordinating connectors such as *although, because, unless,* etc.

Vocabulary.—The vocabulary test of one hundred items was administered orally and individually to each subject during the kindergarten year. This vocabulary test was adapted from one devised by A. F. Watts, British research worker. British items such as *teahouse* were changed to *restaurant* or *cafe.* All items on the vocabulary test were questions which Watts asserts an average child of the age of eight and one-half should know. Typical questions are those in which the questioner asks, "What am I touching?" as he places his finger on his nose, eyebrows, or elbow. The British version is included in Watts' book, *The Language and Mental Development of Children.*[25] This vocabulary test, weighted equally with the average of four or more years of teachers' ratings, became the basis for selection of the two groups of subjects at the extremes of language ability.[26]

Intelligence.—In the second grade of the Oakland primary schools, the Kuhlmann-Anderson Intelligence Test is administered to all pupils. Where a discrepancy appears between a pupil's score and the teacher's observations of the pupil's intellectual performance in class, further testing is carried out with another form of the same test or the individual Stanford-Binet Scale. Intelligence tests are also repeated in later grades. All these scores were available for the subjects in this study. Subjects who had moved to nearby school districts by this time were also tested with the same tests.

Use of subordinators.—Watts has devised a test calling for the completion of unfinished sentences broken off at the point where a subordinating connector has just been introduced.[27] The correct

---

[25]Watts, *op. cit.,* pp. 280-283.
[26]Both scores were converted to standard scores and then the two scores were averaged. Subjects two or more standard deviations from the mean were classified as high or low in language.
[27]Watts, *op. cit.,* pp. 302-305.

completion has to be selected from among four phrases offered as possibles. An example follows:

I shall not be able to do my arithmetic unless
a) my exercise book is full.
b) you help me.
c) multiplication is very hard.
d) I forget my tables.

Beginning with grade five, this test was administered yearly to all subjects in the present research.

Ratings and Indices

In addition to the techniques and tests already described, six important ratings or indices were procured for all subjects in the study. These indices quantified teachers' estimates of the subjects' language ability, reading ability, writing ability, socioeconomic status, health, and school attendance.

Teachers' ratings of subjects.—For each year of the study, the teachers of the subjects rated them on selected language factors: (1) amount of language; (2) quality of vocabulary; (3) skill in communication; (4) organization, purpose, and control of language; (5) wealth of ideas; and (6) quality of listening. Inasmuch as this scale, along with the vocabulary test, comprised the basis on which the investigator selected the high and low groups representing the extremes of language ability, the scale merits particular mention. The reader's attention is directed to the fact that for each subject seven of these rating scales were available, one from each of seven teachers. In grades K through three the average score for the first four ratings was given equal weight with the vocabulary scores in order to determine the two groups at the extremes of language ability. In grades four through six the ratings for all the years to date were used.

Index of reading ability.—For each child, complete cumulative records of reading progress were kept from year to year, listing the pre-primers, primers, readers, enrichment or supplementary readers, and recreational reading completed. In order to reduce the multiplicity of reading to a manageable score, the investigator assigned numerical weights to each of these books during the primary school years. The final sum for each subject, called the reading index, represented scores ranging from 3.5 for one child still unable to read much of anything at the end of the grade three to 50 for the most accomplished reader in the group.

Beginning in the fourth grade, all subjects were tested on the Stanford Achievement Test which includes word and paragraph meaning. Later other reading tests were sometimes administered.

Index of writing ability.—Beginning with the third grade, a sample of the subjects' writing was taken annually under standard conditions for all. A picture, somewhat complicated as to content, was shown to all subjects; they were permitted to write until they gave obvious evidence of having exhausted their fund of writing energy for this particular picture.

Two judges, both teachers of writing, classified the samples of writing into five categories as follows:

I *Superior*
1. Uses well-constructed sentences
2. Employs a variety of sentence patterns
3. Uses phrases and clauses skillfully
4. Uses relational (transitional) words—*yet, however, since,* etc.—to bridge the parts of his writing
5. Has well-organized ideas
6. Gives time and place
7. Includes title
8. Employs vigorous verbs
9. Employs a vivid, picture-evoking vocabulary, specific rather than general
10. Uses correct spelling and punctuation
11. Relates picture content to past or present experiences
12. Shows awareness of reader
13. Achieves clarity of content
14. Has proportion, development, and completeness

II *Good*
1. Uses limited sentence patterns
2. Uses few, if any, relational words
3. Begins to organize but strays from basis of organization
4. Displays monotonous vocabulary
5. Uses reasonably correct spelling and punctuation
6. Interprets only the obvious, barely achieving interpretation
7. Fails to be specific; tends to generalities

III *Inferior*

1. Employs weak or faulty sentence structure, indicating lack of understanding
2. Uses no relational words
3. Makes no attempt to organize
4. Employs a limited vocabulary
5. Uses poor spelling and faulty punctuation
6. Gives no interpretation or at best an unrelated one
7. Tends to be fragmentary or, in longer writing, disjointed or formless

IV *Illiterate*

1. Achieves only faulty sentences
2. Employs occasional groups of related words
3. Fails to complete some words
4. Uses lists of words, related to the picture
5. Uses barely comprehensible language and spelling

V *Primitive*

1. Resorts to pictures or drawings
2. Uses meaningless symbols or tangles of letters
3. Lists words either unrelated or only partially related to the picture

The classification assigned to the subjects' writing was then used for a study of its relation to achievement in reading, oral language, and other measures of the subjects' use of language.

School attendance.—Because the financing of education in California is based upon average daily attendance in school districts, strict records of attendance are kept in all schools. For each subject in the study it was possible to locate an exact record of the number of days present in school and to relate this index of school attendance to such matters as reading, writing, and speaking ability.

Socioeconomic status.—The occupation of both parents (or of legal guardians) was determined for all subjects and classified according to the Minnesota Scale for Paternal Occupations. On this scale subjects are ranked in the following categories of paternal occupation:

I Professional
II Semiprofessional

III Clerical, Skilled Trades, Retail Business
IV Farming
V Semiskilled Occupations
VI Slightly Skilled Trades
VII Day Labor

The Minnesota Scale for Paternal Occupations is published by the Institute of Child Welfare, University of Minnesota, Minneapolis.

SUMMARY

The plans and arrangements for a longitudinal study of a representative sample of subjects have been described. In addition to the complete sample of 338 kindergarten pupils, two special subgroups were identified for intensive study: a group of 30 subjects exceptionally high in language ability and a group of 24 subjects exceptionally low in language ability. These two groups were selected by weighting equally (1) the vocabulary test administered in the kindergarten and (2) the combined score of the ratings by all the teachers who taught the subjects in the kindergarten and elementary school years. These two measures have been converted to standard scores and given equal weight with a mean of 50 and a standard deviation of ten. All those subjects two standard deviations or more from the mean were selected to comprise the two special groups representing the two extremes of language ability. The two criteria—vocabulary and teacher ratings—were chosen in lieu of any other established standards of proficiency with language. One purpose of this research is to locate such standards through empirical evidence.

The techniques and procedures by which the data were collected and analyzed have been presented under four headings: new methods of analysis; methods based on previous research; tests; and ratings or indices.

In the next section, the findings, resulting from the application of these procedures and techniques, are presented under headings related to the purposes of this research.

TABLE 1

Amount of Language: Total Group of Subjects

Measures of Central Tendency and Variability for Words, Communication Units, and Mazes

Grade	Total number of words in transcript		Communication units		Total number of words in communication units		Average number of words per communication unit		Mazes		Total number of words in mazes		Average number of words per maze	
	M	σ	M	σ	M	σ	M	σ	M	σ	M	σ	M	σ
Kindergarten (N=338)	555.48	478.00	99.74	28.07	487.13	391.22	4.81	1.33	25.31	21.42	68.35	67.24	2.58	0.97
Grade One (N=260)	618.66	314.62	92.00	30.33	557.00	260.43	6.05	1.37	23.15	16.97	61.66	54.19	2.48	0.92
Grade Two (N=261)	581.00	295.87	103.50	55.00	529.40	263.34	6.57	1.18	20.60	15.23	51.60	32.53	2.39	0.92
Grade Three (N=259)	778.40	383.31	109.80	37.74	730.50	342.75	6.65	1.81	20.50	16.21	47.90	40.56	2.45	1.34
Grade Four (N=246)	945.15	489.80	111.14	48.27	877.95	452.65	7.70	1.26	31.49	21.22	67.20	51.66	2.05	0.44
Grade Five (N=243)	1331.51	671.64	153.62	67.91	1232.87	615.31	7.89	1.10	45.68	33.33	98.64	86.20	2.03	0.41
Grade Six (N=236)	1507.93	759.61	163.37	72.15	1394.31	687.89	8.37	1.25	52.38	42.17	113.62	107.24	2.07	0.41

Chapter Two

FINDINGS

The previous chapter has described the research design and the procedures for gathering and analyzing evidence on children's developing use and control of language. The present chapter deals with the results of those procedures. The evidence on *fluency* will be presented first; next in order will follow the findings on *effectiveness and control* of language, the *functions* accomplished by the subjects' use of language, and the *interrelations* among the various aspects of language.

FLUENCY

Readiness and smoothness of speech are part of proficiency with oral language. A parallel fluency appears in the writing of such men as Shelley or Churchill, poets and statesmen whose written and oral language excels that of the average person. Obviously fluency with words unaccompanied by organization or coherence can be a vice rather than a virtue, but the ability to find words with which to express oneself—and to find them readily—is normally one mark of success with language. The initial examination of the data in this study, therefore, will examine the subjects' fluency.

The findings on fluency are drawn from four sources: (1) the amount of language uttered by all subjects; (2) the subjects' freedom from mazes; (3) the extent of their vocabularies; and (4) their manner of speaking as quantified by two classifications of linguistic style, the ratings for fluency-hesitancy and for readiness-slowness of response.

For sheer amount of language—regardless of its quality or coherence—transcripts of the children's interviews in the seven-year period show a range from a total of two words to a total of 4,129 words. Table 1 shows the means and measures of variability for total number of words in the transcripts. As indicated by the increasing mean in column one, the subjects speak more words in each of the succeeding years, increasing notably (except for the low group) in grades four, five, and six. During these seven years they also increase the

29

TABLE 2

Amount of Language: Highest Group of Subjects
Measures of Central Tendency and Variability for Words, Communication Units, and Mazes

Grade	Total number of words in transcript		Communication units		Total number of words in communication units		Average number of words per communication unit		Mazes		Total number of words in mazes		Average number of words per maze	
	M	σ	M	σ	M	σ	M	σ	M	σ	M	σ	M	σ
Kindergarten (N=30)	704.60	363.72	105.60	36.06	640.00	333.46	5.76	1.53	23.81	15.10	64.60	61.70	2.61	1.48
Grade One (N=30)	715.60	334.76	93.00	31.73	661.40	296.43	6.89	1.39	20.27	12.13	54.20	52.90	2.23	0.67
Grade Two (N=30)	860.60	348.89	112.50	31.84	803.40	316.44	7.04	1.18	16.53	12.42	57.20	42.60	2.32	0.63
Grade Three (N=30)	930.20	399.70	111.70	34.84	883.90	369.97	7.73	1.33	15.29	9.37	46.30	37.80	2.18	0.60
Grade Four (N=25)	1237.68	507.25	133.32	47.74	1170.48	457.28	8.77	1.08	31.76	23.37	67.20	59.66	2.03	0.37
Grade Five (N=25)	1404.92	545.34	150.40	51.81	1332.24	505.57	8.85	0.95	35.00	24.07	72.68	55.54	1.99	0.31
Grade Six (N=25)	1705.76	653.61	170.12	61.64	1617.60	610.16	9.48	1.12	43.80	25.62	88.16	62.83	1.97	0.24

TABLE 2 (cont.)

Amount of Language: Lowest Group of Subjects
Measures of Central Tendency and Variability for Words, Communication Units, and Mazes

Grade	Total number of words in transcript		Communication units		Total number of words in communication units		Average number of words per communication unit		Mazes		Total number of words in mazes		Average number of words per maze	
	M	σ	M	σ	M	σ	M	σ	M	σ	M	σ	M	σ
Kindergarten (N=22)	453.10	363.81	87.40	48.20	399.10	319.51	4.18	1.29	28.03	22.51	54.00	63.40	2.46	1.11
Grade One (N=22)	432.00	244.91	69.10	23.43	365.00	190.41	4.89	1.36	27.15	21.35	67.00	72.70	2.65	1.52
Grade Two (N=22)	553.60	283.03	89.80	36.34	495.50	252.57	5.49	1.18	23.62	16.27	58.10	53.20	2.52	0.94
Grade Three (N=22)	642.90	346.08	90.10	28.51	574.60	305.61	6.08	1.82	23.01	16.91	68.30	55.50	3.17	2.26
Grade Four (N=24)	681.39	303.45	93.61	32.08	615.00	274.43	6.42	1.20	29.61	18.11	66.39	47.56	2.16	0.49
Grade Five (N=24)	989.25	304.45	128.96	30.26	897.54	265.86	6.90	0.93	41.92	25.71	91.71	73.78	2.03	0.44
Grade Six (N=24)	1179.00	738.92	144.79	77.55	1067.12	663.55	7.19	0.88	46.46	35.03	111.88	109.04	2.27	0.57

number of communication units and the average number of words spoken in each of those communication units.

Table 2 shows the data accumulated for the high and low subgroups. On total number of words the high subgroup obviously exceeded the low group in every year of the study. Both groups made a steady increase from year to year in the average number of words for each unit of communication, but the high group consistently exceeded the low group by one or two words. The range in performance as shown by the standard deviation for words per communication unit was about the same for both groups.

The mazes show a different pattern. In the first four years (kindergarten through third grade), the total group and the high subgroup show a steady decrease in the number of mazes and words in mazes from year to year. However, for the low subgroup, *the average number of words per maze* increases. By comparing the high and low groups in Table 2 the reader will see that two contrary trends are operating among the subjects. In grades K through three those who are rated as skillful with language reducing both their incidence of mazes and the number of words per maze: their number of mazes decreases 35 percent; their variability on words per maze decreases more than 50 percent. On the other hand, those rated less skillful with language are increasing both the average number of words and the variability of the number of words they use in each maze whereas the number of mazes they are using is decreasing only half as rapidly (an 18 percent decrease).

In the three subsequent years (fourth grade through sixth grade), mazes must be viewed in relation to the increasing amount of language (total words in transcript). After the kindergarten year the low group exceeds the high group on number of mazes and average number of words per maze. Although the total group and the high subgroup do in fact increase their incidence of mazes, in relation to the *total number of words* they continue to have far less a proportion of mazes than does the low subgroup. The following figures, computed directly from Tables 1 and 2, show how important it is to examine not only raw figures on mazes and words in mazes but also their relation to total volume of language and communication units:

	Percentage of Words in Mazes in Relation to Total Words			Percentage of Mazes Occurring in Relation to Communication Units[1]		
Grade	High Subgroup	Low Subgroup	Total Group	High Subgroup	Low Subgroup	Total Group
K	9.17	11.92	12.30	22.55	32.07	25.38
1st	7.57	15.51	9.97	21.80	39.29	25.16
2nd	6.65	10.49	8.88	14.69	26.30	19.90
3rd	4.98	10.62	6.15	13.69	25.54	18.67
4th	5.43	9.74	7.11	23.82	31.63	28.33
5th	5.17	9.27	7.41	23.27	32.51	29.74
6th	5.17	9.49	7.53	25.75	32.09	32.06

Although at the present we have only seven years by which to judge mazes, we may see from the data in Table 2 that the high group is reducing both the number and the variability of words per maze whereas the low group, on this obstacle to fluency, is more erratic in its performance. Furthermore, the high proportion of mazes and words in mazes for the low subgroup occurs in spite of the fact that communication units and words per communication unit have a lower incidence in this subgroup than in the high subgroup. In other words, the members of the low subgroup say less and many of them have more difficulty in saying it.

Studying the data for words and mazes, however, is not sufficient. We must also see how the subjects behave when they use words in syntactic units that communicate meaning. For this we turn to a scrutiny of the communication units. For the number of communication units, Figure 1 shows the median for the total group and the median and interquartile ranges for the two subgroups (grades one through three). The overlapping is fairly large. However, the means and the quartiles of the high and low subgroups never cross; the high group always maintains its lead on amount of communication units. This is particularly impressive in view of the later finding that the high group is using more subordination than the low group, thus reducing the number of communication units by combining them in complex fashion. *Even so,* the high group still exceeds the low group in number of communication units.

From one school year to another, the amount of meaningful language or communication units increases slowly and gradually through-

---

[1]Note the phenomena of U-shaped curves with third grade showing (with one exception) the lowest percentages for subgroups as well as for the total group.

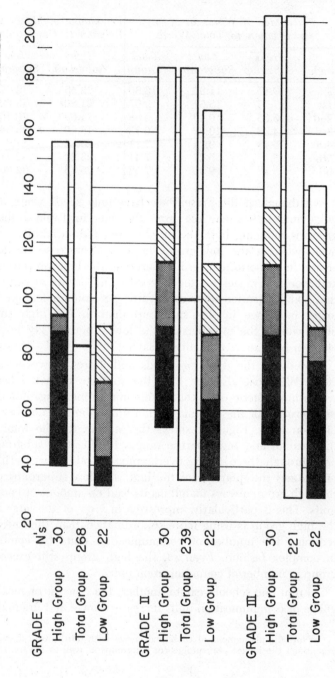

Figure 1

Number of Communication Units for Grades One, Two, and Three
Median for Total Group
Median and Interquartile Range for Two Subgroups

Wide band indicates median ; quartiles are indicated by cross hatch

out the primary school years and then spurts forward at the fifth grade level. In this respect the low subgroup moves forward much like the high subgroup and the total group, showing an appreciable jump in meaningful language at grade five. Children high in language ability maintain their initial superiority over those low in language ability. In respect to mazes, members of both groups continue to have trouble with expression from year to year, but those in the high group are more fluent and are gaining greater control over this fluency.

In respect to vocabulary, it seems logical that children with large and readily accessible vocabularies would find expression easier than those with limited vocabularies. Certainly vocabulary ought to be included in any examination of verbal fluency. In this research, evidence both of quantity and quality of vocabulary is available from four sources. First, we have for all subjects their position on the vocabulary test administered in the kindergarten. (See page 23.) Second, for all subjects, there are the teachers' ratings on vocabulary, one subsection of the Teachers' Rating Scale. (See page 24.) Third, for the two subgroups we have their vocabulary classified according to frequency of use in the English language. (See page 22.) Lastly, we have the type-token ratios for the two subgroups, indicating the diversification of their vocabulary. (See pages 22-23.)

On the Kindergarten Vocabulary Test of 100 items, the subjects' scores vary from 3 to 83 with a mean of 50.46. Table 3 presents the mean and standard deviation for this test, and Figure 2 presents the frequency distribution in graphic form. For British children at the same

TABLE 3

Measures of Central Tendency and Variability on Two Measures
Means and Standard Deviations for the Distributions
of Vocabulary and Teacher Rating
Kindergarten Year

	N	Mean	σ
Scores on Kindergarten Vocabulary Test of 100 items	320	50.46	15.35
Teacher rating.................	317	3.27	0.84

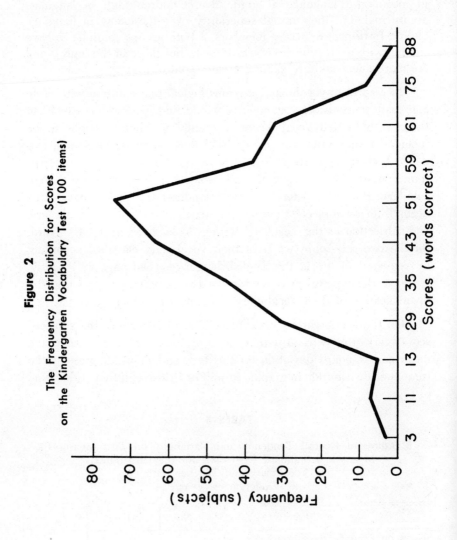

Figure 2

The Frequency Distribution for Scores
on the Kindergarten Vocabulary Test (100 items)

age, Watts, who devised this test, gives a score of 53 as a norm.[1] He demonstrates that the vocabulary in his test does sample fairly evenly the first, second, third, fourth, fifth, and sixth thousands of most commonly used words in the *American Teacher's Word Book* by E. L. Thorndike. Inasmuch as the 100 words in his vocabulary test are fairly evenly spread throughout the list of the six thousand most common words, Watts considers it reasonable to estimate that the probable size of a child's vocabulary—within a 10 percent error—is sixty times the number right on his test. In accordance with this reasoning, the subjects in the present study—at the kindergarten level—vary in vocabulary from 180 to about 5,000 words with 3,000 words as an average.[2] In comparison with similar results by other research workers such as Smith, these figures seem valid.[3] The size of the total vocabulary for children of this age is still a controversial issue, however, and some investigators do not agree with Smith's and Watts' estimates or methods of arriving at them. However, in terms of extent of vocabulary, the central tendency and variance support the hypothesis that the subjects in this study represent a larger universe of children.

In this research, the high and low subgroups were selected by an equally weighted combination of this vocabulary test and the average of all the teachers' ratings on language. The median score on the vocabulary test for the high group was 67 and for the low group, 35. For the purposes of validation as well as for evidence on vocabulary, the investigator computed the medians for the low and high groups on the section of the teachers' rating scale which dealt with vocabulary. The median for the high group is 4.51 and for the low group, 1.94.

The frequency of occurrence of English words has been determined and made available in *The Teacher's Word Book of 30,000 Words*.[4] Through a frequency classification of the words used by the low and high subgroups, we can contrast these two groups on range of vocabulary. How many commonly used words appear in

---

[1]Watts, *op. cit.*, p. 50. (See p. 6.) Watts does not describe his sample.

[2]The lowest figure, 180, may seem exceptional, but this was a child who at the time of the test spoke Chinese and only a small amount of English.

[3]M. E. Smith, "An Investigation of the Development of the Sentence and the Extent of Vocabulary in Young Children," *Child Welfare*, 3: 5 (1926). Iowa City: University of Iowa.

[4]Thorndike and Lorge, *op. cit.* (See p. 22.)

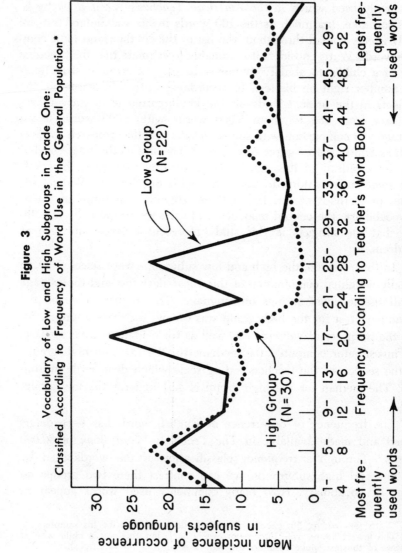

Figure 3

Vocabulary of Low and High Subgroups in Grade One:
Classified According to Frequency of Word Use in the General Population*

*According to E. L. Thorndike and I. Lorge, The Teacher's Word Book of 30,000 Words
(New York: Teachers College, Columbia University, Bureau of Publications, 1944).

their spoken language? Such words will be among the first and second thousands in *The Teacher's Word Book*. How many unusual words will they use? Such words will be among the higher thousands reported in *The Teacher's Word Book*. Although allowances will need to be made for the fact that the Thorndike-Lorge count in *The Teacher's Word Book* is based on written materials, the classification should still be revealing. A few words like *television*, uncommon at the time of the Thorndike-Lorge count, will also affect the tally. Nevertheless, the results should conform to the general behavior of word frequency rather than to exceptions. Figure 3 depicts graphically the differences in vocabulary between the low and high groups when their words are classified according to frequency of occurrence among the population at large.

It is noteworthy but logical that both high and low groups use almost the same number of words from the first 12,000 most commonly used words; then the low group shows a higher incidence of words from the 13,000 to 33,000 categories, and thereafter the high group is gaining ascendancy.

For diversity of vocabulary the type-token ratio is one measure. When the number of words in the language samples are kept equal, subjects using only a few words repetitiously receive lower scores than those using a widely varied choice of words. In Figures 4a and 4b the ratios of the low and high subgroups are shown in decremental curves. Those curves were determined by dividing the total number of words in each subject's transcript into segments of equal length (100 words). Then for each segment the new words that had not appeared before in any preceding segment were counted. This is necessary in order to control the comparison. Total number of words in a transcript ought not to be compared inasmuch as subjects who used the most words would be penalized if the types (number of different words) were divided by the tokens (total number of words).

In the primary grades the frequency and diversity measures did not discriminate notably between the low and high subgroups. Figures 4a and 4b show that except for the larger number of words used by the high group, both groups reveal the same incidence of new words in each new segment of 100 words. In the case of the type-token ratio, the fault lies in the particular language situation sampled in this research. In this research, the subjects are viewing

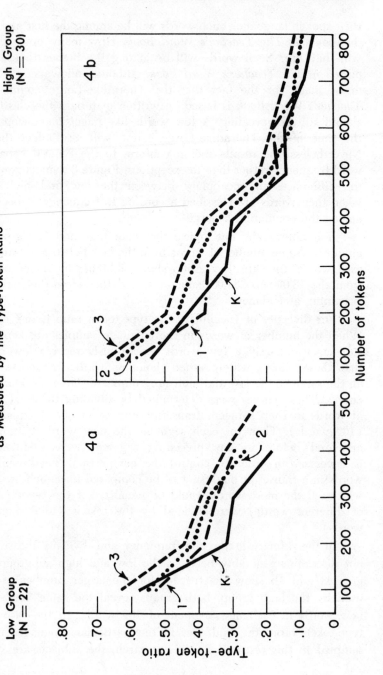

Figure 4

Diversity of Vocabulary for Low and High Subgroups
as Measured by the Type-Token Ratio

six new pictures by the time they reach the third, fourth, and fifth hundred words. Each picture stimulates, alike in low or high subgroups, a new vocabulary. In a different language sample, the type-token ratio would discriminate between the low and the high groups and in later years of this longitudinal research will prove a useful tool for the longer oral statements as well as the writing of the subjects. Likewise, the Thorndike-Lorge frequencies either do not adapt themselves well to spoken language or the difference in "height" of vocabulary is not sufficiently marked among elementary school children—even though they differ in general skill with language. This measure, also, is adversely influenced by the vocabulary stimulus of the succession of new pictures used in the present research design. In later years of this longitudinal study, this measure too will very likely be useful.

When all four vocabulary measures are examined together, however, it is clear that the expected superiority of the high subgroup is consistent. To whatever extent vocabulary is a factor in fluency, those with language ability manifest the greater variety and exactness of vocabulary.

Whether or not mere amount of language contributes to fluency, or whether or not vocabulary contributes to fluency, further evidence of this fluency factor lies in the way oral language actually operates. In this study classifications of language style are based on the recorded voices of the subjects in the two subgroups, and in two of these classifications of oral language style, fluency is featured:

fluent, smooth	to	hesitant, faltering, labored
ready and full in response	to	meager and slow in response

To find out whether or not those subjects low or high in language ability tended to be different from the total group in respect to these two classifications, the investigation employed the chi-square test. Rather than assume the null hypothesis or to estimate theoretical frequencies, the investigator used the table of random numbers to select an equal number of subjects from the total sample. Those members from the total sample, selected thus at random, were then classified by the same methods used for the low and high subgroups, and the resulting scores were used to replace theoretical frequencies in the computation of chi-square.

In these classifications the high subgroup is significantly more fluent than the total sample. However, their readiness of response does not prove to differ from the random group. The low group proves to be more hesitant than the rest of the subjects in this study, and they are somewhat more slow of response. The results need to be considered only tentative inasmuch as cells with less than six cases occur frequently among the results for the random group.[5]

SUMMARY ON FLUENCY

To summarize the evidence on fluency, then, these subjects, over a period of seven years, increase the amount of language they use in the same controlled situation and, by reducing the proportion and size of their mazes, gain an increase of smoothness in their expression. Those who are rated high on language ability appear to be superior to the total sample for fluency and readiness of response, and they use more words in each year of the study than do those low in language ability. The high group also has a larger, more varied, and more readily accessible vocabulary. These subjects reduce the incidence of their mazes by 35 percent over the first four years and are also during these four years reducing the total number of words in mazes and the average number of words in mazes. The low group, on the other hand, despite the fact that it uses fewer words, is increasing the total number of words and average number of words in mazes over the same period (kindergarten through third grade), even though it is reducing the incidence of mazes by 18 percent. In grades four through six, where the amount of language increases notably, the high group consistently has a smaller *proportion* of mazes and words in mazes than the low group and consistently uses fewer words per maze. Lastly, there is a significant tendency for all subjects in the sample to maintain a consistent relative position in the total group when fluency (as measured by the average number of words per communication unit) is measured from year to year.

It would appear that members of the low group experience more difficulty in using and controlling the patterns of English syntax and therefore involve themselves in more language tangles or mazes per volume of spoken language than do members of the high group. The mazes certainly reduce fluency, whatever the cause for mazes may

---

[5] The statistics, not included here, are available from the writer.

be. The low group says less, has more difficulty in saying it, and has less vocabulary with which to express what it says.

EFFECTIVENESS AND CONTROL

Words and readiness with them are one part of power over language, but unless a speaker or writer imposes a purposeful order upon such fluency, his language is likely to be prolix drivel or chatter. Consequently the findings bearing upon effectiveness and control of language, presented in this section, are highly important to the purpose of this study. Evidence on effectiveness and control has been drawn together from a number of sources:

. . . ability to use and vary the structural patterns of English (First Level Analysis)
. . . dexterity in varying elements within the structural patterns (Second Level Analysis)
. . . competence with reading and writing
. . . coherence through the use of subordination
. . . coherence through use of subordinating connectives
. . . coherence through control of mazes
. . . coherence of spoken style
. . . mastery of conventional usage and grammar
. . . ability to express tentative thinking by means of provisional or conditional statements

All in all, at least nine measures in this study will provide evidence on the subjects' effectiveness and control. Logically these measures provide a reasonably comprehensive description of language effectiveness and control.

First Level Analysis: Ability to use and vary the structural patterns of English

The subjects' oral language was analyzed for evidence on ability to use and vary the basic structural patterns of English. Each communication unit was classified and tallied as shown in Tables 4a and 4b. Because the high group used more language, the results in Tables 4a and 4b have been computed in percent of total amount of language in order to make the two groups comparable. Percents have been rounded out to two figures. The tables yield the following evidence:

TABLE 4a

First Level Analysis: High Group
Relative Proportions of Structural Patterns
Showing Median, First Quartile, and Third Quartile
According to Percent of Pattern Used in Total Transcripts for Seven Years

N = 25

Pattern

High	1 2			1 2 4			1 ② 5			1 2 3 4			1 2 4 6			1 ② 1		
N=25	Q_1	Md	Q_3	Q_1	Md	Q_3	Q_1	Md	Q_3	Q_1	Md	Q_3	Q_1	Md	Q_3	Q_1	Md	Q_3
K	21	24	21	30	27	29	10	11	13	0	1	1	0	0	1	2	3	5
1	20	21	21	36	37	33	10	16	15	0	0	1	0	0	1	2	3	5
2	19	21	23	33	34	32	15	17	18	0	0	1	0	0	0	3	7	7
3	22	20	24	38	38	33	12	17	17	0	0	1	0	0	1	6	5	6
4	25	27	24	38	36	36	20	17	17	0	2	2	0	0	1	4	5	5
5	25	28	27	41	35	32	13	18	16	1	1	1	0	0	1	2	3	4
6	29	28	29	38	39	38	16	15	16	1	1	2	0	1	1	1	2	3

Grade

Pattern

High	WQ			Passive			Partial		
N=25	Q_1	Md	Q_3	Q_1	Md	Q_3	Q_1	Md	Q_3
K	0	0	1	0	0	0	38	34	30
1	0	0	1	0	0	1	32	24	24
2	0	0	1	0	0	1	25	21	22
3	0	0	1	0	0	1	21	19	19
4	0	0	1	0	0	1	14	13	13
5	0	0	0	1	1	1	15	13	18
6	0	0	0	0	1	1	14	14	11

Grade

TABLE 4b

First Level Analysis: Low Group
Relative Proportions of Structural Patterns
Showing Median, First Quartile, and Third Quartile
According to Percent of Pattern Used in Total Transcripts for Seven Years

$$N = 24$$

Pattern

Low	1 2			1 2 4			1 ② 5			1 2 3 4			1 2 4 6			1 ② 1		
N=24	Q_1	Md	Q_3	Q_1	Md	Q_3	Q_1	Md	Q_3	Q_1	Md	Q_3	Q_1	Md	Q_3	Q_1	Md	Q_3
K	19	23	21	22	26	28	5	6	9	0	0	1	0	0	0	0	0	1
1	20	25	23	17	26	32	6	7	10	0	0	1	0	0	0	0	0	3
2	25	25	21	27	31	32	9	10	11	0	0	1	0	0	0	1	4	3
3	24	24	24	27	33	30	10	10	12	0	0	2	0	0	1	1	2	4
4	23	27	27	37	36	34	12	11	14	0	0	1	0	0	0	0	2	3
5	26	28	26	37	34	33	11	12	11	0	1	2	0	0	1	3	4	4
6	31	28	31	34	36	34	14	12	11	1	2	3	0	0	0	1	2	3

Grade

Pattern

Low	WQ			Passive			Partial		
N=24	Q_1	Md	Q_3	Q_1	Md	Q_3	Q_1	Md	Q_3
K	0	0	3	0	0	0	54	45	38
1	0	0	1	0	0	0	58	42	32
2	0	0	1	0	0	0	38	30	30
3	0	0	0	0	0	1	37	31	27
4	0	0	0	0	0	1	27	23	20
5	0	0	0	0	0	1	24	22	21
6	0	0	0	0	1	1	20	18	18

Grade

. . . The low group uses many more partial communication units (units that are incomplete, for whatever reason) than the high group. For both groups the percent of partials decreases with chronological age.

. . . The high group uses more linking verb patterns (1 ② 5).

. . . The (1) ② 1 pattern (*there is, it is, there are*) increases and then decreases for the high group; it is never used very much by the low group.

. . . The outer complement (1 2 4 6) is used only by the highest of the high group.

. . . The inner complement (1 2 3 4) is seldom used by either group and appears not to be a frequent pattern in English, certainly not among children in this study. The incidence of use for this pattern is slightly more frequent for the high group.

. . . The passive pattern is employed only slightly by the high group, although examination of the transcripts shows that subjects in the low subgroup use the passive occasionally, even as early as kindergarten.

. . . Except for pattern 1 ② 5 and the use of partials, differences between high and low groups are not notable.

Examination of the transcripts shows that *some* subjects in the low subgroup know and use all nine patterns in the kindergarten.

Second Level Analysis: Dexterity in varying elements within the structural patterns

All these subjects—high, random, or low—use the relatively few structural patterns of the English language. Thus structural pattern reveals less remarkable differences than does dexterity of substitution *within* the patterns. The important differences show up in the substitution of word groups for single words, in the choice and arrangement of movable syntactic elements, in variety of nominals, and in strategies with predication. Here the subjects' differences are much greater, as may be seen in Tables 5, 6, and 7.

MOVABLES

Essential sentence elements, those determining the structural patterns in the First Level Analysis, occupy fixed positions. In English, word order determines meaning. English speakers can say *Mary ate*

TABLE 5

Dexterity in Varying Elements within Structural Patterns: Movables
Median of High and Low Groups in Percent of Various Movables Used

High Group N = 25   Low Group N = 24

Grade	Group	Words	Phrases	Clauses	Multiples
K	High	36.2	45.3	9.9	5.0
	Low	34.6	54.3	5.9	0.0
1	High	35.7	47.6	9.6	3.0
	Low	39.5	47.8	6.1	0.0
2	High	36.1	49.4	12.7	4.4
	Low	41.6	45.9	7.0	0.6
3	High	41.3	45.1	10.2	3.1
	Low	37.6	48.4	10.7	2.0
4	High	34.7	47.8	11.3	5.1
	Low	38.6	47.7	5.0	2.2
5	High	35.9	47.4	11.1	4.7
	Low	38.2	46.9	9.8	3.2
6	High	37.0	49.4	10.7	4.6
	Low	37.9	48.0	3.8	3.3

the rhubarb (1 2 4), but they cannot say *The rhubarb ate Mary* and make sense. Even in poetic inversion they risk misunderstanding. English has no 4 2 1 pattern. The essential sentence elements, then, have a fixed order in our language.

There are, however, some less essential elements which are relatively unfixed, adverbial modifiers like *usually, in the meantime,* and *if you don't really like it.* In this study these have been classified as words, phrases, clauses, and multiple movable constructions (movables within movables such as *holding the clowns in his hands* or *whoever in the excitement manages to keep from laughing*). The high and low groups show little difference in the use of words and phrases as movables, but as will be seen by their medians in Table 5, the high group consistently shows a greater repertoire *of clauses*

TABLE 6

Dexterity in Varying Elements within Structural Patterns:
Nominals Used as Subjects

Median of High and Low Groups in Percent of Varieties of Nominals

High Group N = 25   Low Group N = 24

Grade	Group	Nouns	Pronouns	Verbals	Infinitives	Prep. Phrases	Clauses
K	High	18.8	80.8	0	0	0	0
	Low	18.8	81.2	0	0	0	0
1	High	23.7	76.0	0	0	0	0
	Low	25.8	74.2	0	0	0	0
2	High	22.5	77.5	0	0	0	0
	Low	24.0	76.0	0	0	0	0
3	High	23.2	76.8	0	0	0	0
	Low	26.0	74.0	0	0	0	0
4	High	18.6	81.4	0	0	0	0
	Low	23.1	76.9	0	0	0	0
5	High	17.7	81.3	0	0	0	0
	Low	27.4	72.6	0	0	0	0
6	High	24.2	75.5	0	0	0	0
	Low	23.2	76.8	0	0	0	0

and multiples used as movable elements in the sentence. In order
to make direct comparison possible between the two groups, the
number of movable types in their transcripts has been converted to
percent of totals.

NOMINALS USED AS SUBJECTS

As will be seen by Table 6, high and low groups use nouns (including noun-headed nominal phrases) and pronouns almost exclusively for sentence subjects, and both groups do so in about the same
proportions. The medians for both groups do not, however, reveal
the fact that the high group exceeds the low group in the number of

more complicated constructions used as subjects. The following shows what happens when complicated constructions are tallied:

	High	Low
Verbals	13	1
Infinitives	18	3
Prepositional phrases	5	4
Clauses	28	0
Total	64	8

In the low group, during the years from kindergarten through grade six, there occur only eight instances of subject nominals more complicated than a noun, pronoun, or noun-headed nominal phrase. Of these eight, half are prepositional phrases and none are clauses. The boys in the low group contributed only two of the eight instances (two infinitives).

NOMINALS USED AS COMPLEMENTS

For nominals used as complements the same situation develops. Both groups, as can be seen in Table 7, use nouns, noun-headed nominal phrases, and pronouns as complements with about the same frequency. The difference lies in the use of infinitives and clauses where the high group invariably exceeds the low group.

Because many subjects did not use verbals or prepositional phrases as complements, the median again does not reveal any differences. However, the actual incidences occurring in the two groups for seven years do differ as follows:

	High		Low	
	boys	girls	boys	girls
Verbals	39	49	19	34
Prepositional phrases	57	22	14	26
Total	96	71	33	60
Total (boys and girls)	167		93	

The boys in the low group are the ones who have the smallest repertoire, the least dexterity. Also, in the high group there is the interesting phenomenon of boys exceeding the girls.

TABLE 7

Dexterity in Varying Elements within Structural Patterns:
Nominals Used as Complements

Median of High and Low Groups in Percent of Varieties of Nominals

High Group N = 25   Low Group N = 24

(Complements tallied represent direct and indirect
objects, predicate nominatives, and object complements.)

Grade	Group	Nouns	Pronouns	Verbals	Infinitives	Prep. Phrases	Clauses
K	High	58.6	22.0	0	9.0	0	8.3
	Low	53.6	29.6	0	4.2	0	2.8
1	High	62.4	19.0	0	5.7	0	8.0
	Low	67.8	17.8	0	3.6	0	4.7
2	High	59.6	21.8	0	8.1	0	11.1
	Low	60.8	24.6	0	5.2	0	5.4
3	High	56.5	21.7	0	9.5	0	10.4
	Low	65.5	22.1	0	4.7	0	7.3
4	High	50.7	23.1	0	9.0	0	12.7
	Low	58.1	24.0	0	6.5	0	7.4
5	High	50.8	22.3	0	10.8	0	13.1
	Low	54.0	25.2	0	8.4	0	7.2
6	High	51.9	22.6	0	11.6	0	12.8
	Low	50.6	24.3	0	9.6	0	8.8

NOMINALS USED AS OBJECTS OF PREPOSITIONS AND VERBALS

As in the previous analyses, the high group exceeds the low
group in using any form of nominal except the single noun or pronoun. Nouns amplified by modifiers, compound nouns, clauses, infinitives—all these characterize the high group rather than the low
group. Once again the high boys manifest slightly greater flexibility
than the high girls, and the low boys are more restricted in their
repertoires than are the low girls.

Mastery of conventional usage and grammar

Effectiveness with language often requires an ability to use those conventions characterizing standard English, a term defined by Fries as "a set of language habits in which the major matters of the political, social, economic, educational, religious life of this country are carried on."

> To these language habits is attached a certain social prestige, for the use of them suggests constant relations with those responsible for the important affairs of our communities. It is this set of language habits . . . which is the "standard" not because it is any more correct or more beautiful or more capable than other varieties of English; it is "standard" solely because it is the particular type of English used in the conduct of the important affairs of our people. It is also the type of English used by the *socially acceptable* of most of our communities, and insofar as that is true it has become social or class dialect in the United States.[6]

This definition of standard English requires caution of anyone classifying errors in the speech of a sample such as the children in this research. By this definition, much that school texts emphasize is not error, for superior writers and speakers—even those of prestige—manifest language habits the texts do not accept. In this research, therefore, errors are defined as major deviations in usage and structure, and to identify these major deviations, we have relied upon the research of Leonard,[7] Fries,[8] Marckwardt and Walcott,[9] as well as the recommendations of Pooley.[10]

The analysis of usage and grammar in this research, lengthy enough to be a monograph by itself, has not been completed for all pupils, but a special study of two groups is in final form and is presented here. In tallying nonstandard language, the research analyst soon became aware that use of verbs—and in particular, agreement of verbs with subjects—was the major category of deviation from convention.

---

[6]Charles Carpenter Fries, *American English Grammar* (New York: Appleton-Century-Crofts, 1940), p. 13.

[7]A. Sterling Leonard, *Current English Usage.* English Monographs, No. 1 (Champaign: National Council of Teachers of English, 1932).

[8]Fries, *op. cit.*

[9]Albert H. Marckwardt and Fred G. Walcott, *Facts about English Usage* (New York: Appleton-Century-Crofts, 1938).

[10]Robert C. Pooley, *Teaching English Usage* (New York: Appleton-Century-Crofts, 1946).

For Negro subjects whose parents have migrated from the rural South, using the verb *to be* as it is employed in standard English proved to be twelve times as troublesome as for the Caucasian or Negro subjects whose parents were from the urban California background. Use of present for past tense impresses one as another difficulty to be attacked in the middle grades as well as earlier by these subjects with a rural background. By noting the incidence of southern Negroes' nonstandard usage in relation to those of the northern subjects, one can locate those deviations that will require the greatest help in schools with a number of children similar to this special group. For instance, the use of the nominative pronoun for the possessive shows a large difference between subjects with southern rural and northern urban backgrounds.

Analysis of the nonconventional uses of English (for the total sample, all seven years of this study) shows subject-predicate agreement to be the major source of difficulty with the third person singular verb a particular problem. Consistency in verb tense is another major problem. That sensitivity to the conventions of standard English is related to skill in language shows up in the significant differences on conventional usage in the analysis of spoken style. Statistically the high group is significantly superior to the random group and the low group significantly below the random group.

Ability to express tentative thinking by means of provisional and conditional statements

Ineptness with language is far less serious than malicious perjury or slander, no matter how skillfully or beautifully phrased. The purposes for which human beings use language deserve study. For children's language, as for all language, function is still relatively uncharted. Piaget's disputed analysis of function finds children's language to be primarily egocentric before age seven or eight and more social and analytical in nature after age eleven or twelve. Rugg and others evolved a different set of functional categories: linguistic experimentation, perceptions, self-assertion, and statements of fact, among the most common.[11] Other experimenters have noted requests, threats, criticism, commands, and questions. In the present study expression of tentativeness proved to be a function of language

---

[11]H. Rugg, L. Krueger, and A. Sondergaard, *op. cit.*, p. 9. (See p. 16.)

which distinguished effective and ineffective users of language. Apparently the functions of language are varied and numerous, even in childhood.

Results of all research into function of language depend upon the situation from which language samples are derived. Only when two language investigations sample similar situations will their classification of function be comparable. This points up a limitation of all research into language, including the present study. Until comprehensive long-range research into children's language can be financed or devised, we cannot sample the same subjects over a long-range dimension of time nor can we record samples of the subjects' language *in a wide variety of situations*. In the present research, the language sample was secured in an interview situation identical for all subjects. In such a context, opportunities for such functions as threats, commands, or deception are negligible. In another situation, the findings on vocabulary, usage, and style might differ considerably; certainly the functions of language would vary.

Despite the limitations expressed above, the analysis of linguistic function in this research does reveal one fact of considerable import. Those subjects who proved to have the greatest power over language—by every measure that could be applied, not just by the combined Teachers' Rating Scale and Vocabulary Test—were *the subjects who most frequently used language to express tentativeness*. Supposition, hypotheses, and conditional statements occur much less frequently in the language of subjects lacking skill in language.

The low subgroup furnishes only a few examples of this use of language whereas the high subgroup uses language in this way from the kindergarten year through the sixth grade, employing such words as *perhaps* and *maybe* more often than do the subjects who have difficulty in expressing themselves. These most capable speakers often use such expressions as the following:

It might be a gopher, but I'm not sure.

That, I *think*, is in Africa.

But maybe they don't have any dogs in Alaska.

I'm not exactly sure where that is. It looks like it might be at school.

That's white grass—unless there's snow or the sun is reflecting.

The child with less power over language appears to be less flexible in his thinking, is not often capable of seeing more than one alternative, and apparently summons up all his linguistic resources merely to make a flat dogmatic statement.

TABLE 8

Functions of Language: Classification of Low and High Subgroups
in Eight Categories of Language Function
High N = 25   Low N = 24
Figures Represent Averages for Each Group

Functions of language in a sample drawn from oral interview	School Year								Total for four years	
	Grade Three		Four		Five		Six			
	Low	High	Low	High	Low	High	Low	High	Low	High
Statement of facts, perceptions	23	43	25	48	34	49	46	52	128	192
Interpretations	17	26	16	21	19	19	24	34	76	100
Personal associations	0	16	10	17	11	19	13	21	34	73
Tentative statements	3	28	5	31	7	49	12	51	27	159
Generalizations	0	2	3	8	5	13	7	15	15	38
Irrelevancies	8	2	9	7	9	4	8	0	34	13
Questions	1	5	7	3	3	2	5	4	16	14
Figurative language	0	5	3	12	0	11	5	13	8	41

The sample was composed of 70 communication units drawn from the answer on television and on the six pictures for grades three, four, five, and six. The incidence of each function was tallied and averages (means) computed. However, incidences in proportion to amount of language would be an improvement of this present classification.

In addition to the findings on tentativeness, Table 8 shows that relatively few examples of generalization or figurative language appear in the language of these subjects. The situation from which the language samples were drawn was one in which generalization was entirely possible. Equally surprising is the scarcity of figurative language. A few subjects in the high subgroup and in the total group noted that the rounded top of a fence looked like little hills or that a girl about to cry had a face that was clouding up. Yet the situation from which these language samples were drawn offered, it was believed, exceptionally good opportunity for subjects to use figurative language as well as generalizations.

Competence with reading and writing

Several methods of appraising competence in reading and writing were used in this research. The indices of reading and writing, described on pages 24-25, were two methods of appraisal. The subjects' scores on the reading achievement tests represent further methods of appraisal.

READING

In reading, the subjects' progress in the second and third grades of school was assessed by a reading index. The results for both grades two and three fall into a curve very close to a normal curve. A T-Test of the differences between the means of the two groups high and low in language ability shows, as might be expected, a significant difference in favor of the high group.

For children in the primary grades reading is still very often something one is learning in school. Among the third grade subjects, only 36 percent received credit on the Index of Reading Ability for reading children's recreational books of their own choosing. The other 64 percent had not yet progressed beyond the instructional readers used in their schools.[12]

Beginning in grade four and continuing in grades five and six, the Stanford and California Achievement Tests in Reading were administered. Figure 5 presents the scores for the high, random, and low groups as charted for each of these three grades. It shows that those who are proficient in oral language (the basis of group selection) are also those who are superior in reading achievement; in all quartiles, the high subjects are above their chronological age in reading achievement. By grade six they are *all* above their age expectation. The random group, at their median, are just at the level expected of

---

[12]Evidence on the recreational reading of the subjects has been collected for grades four, five, and six but has not yet been studied.

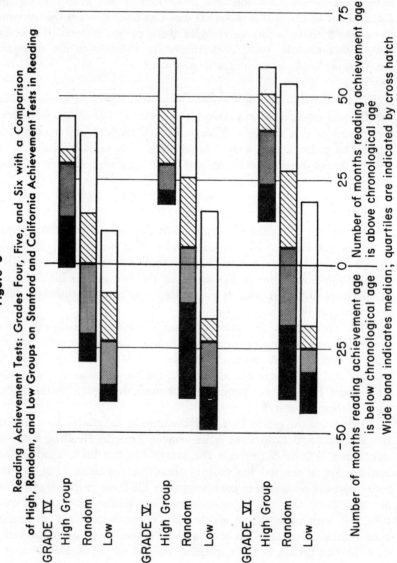

Figure 5

Reading Achievement Tests: Grades Four, Five, and Six with a Comparison of High, Random, and Low Groups on Stanford and California Achievement Tests in Reading

them for their age. Virtually all subjects in the low group are reading significantly below their chronological age in each of the years studied. Only one subject in the low group is consistently above the age-grade mean. The performance of the low group is almost identical in each successive year except that the median and upper quartile are shifting slightly to the left (lower). Considering the shift, and the fact that the high group is shifting to the right (higher), the picture as a whole apparently is a widening reading gap from year to year between those rated high and those rated low in language ability.

WRITING

In grades four, five, and six, a more carefully refined code and scale were developed from the writing index used in grade three. This refined writing scale had five steps, and the papers were rated on a five-point scale. The median rating for the high, random, and low groups for each of grades four, five, and six follows:

Writing Proficiency
Median Rating for High, Random, and Low Groups

	High	Random	Low
Grade Four	Average	Average	Below Average
Grade Five	Average	Average	Below Average
Grade Six	Average	Average	Below Average

An examination of the socioeconomic ratings of the subjects shows that for those in each of the categories, the results on writing were as follows:

Writing Proficiency in Relation to Socioeconomic Status

Socioeconomic Category	Median Rating on Writing (Grades Four, Five, and Six Combined)
I	Average
II	Average
III	Average
IV	Below Average
IV	Below Average
VI	Below Average
VII	Below Average

Coherence through the use of subordination

Effective use of language is more than uttering whatever perceptions or thoughts rise by chance to the surface of expression. The content of effective expression requires organization. In terms of purpose and communicability, the speaker or writer must discriminate among all the materials of expression. Like a good stage director, he must work *behind the scenes,* rapidly placing related materials together, selecting or repressing, providing that all-important logical consecutiveness which enables discourse to "hang together." This implies, also, experience to avoid the pitfalls, to note and to consolidate the successes one has had. This variation in coherence is illustrated in the transcripts of two different first grade subjects. The first child, a boy, organizes his communication by subordinating some ideas to others. The second child, also a boy, reveals no plan of presentation; except for a loose chronology, his content lacks the coherence and emphasis necessary to communicate successfully to another person. He is not fully aware of dependent clauses as a way to order and communicate his ideas.

SUBJECT MANUEL:

Well, I was climbing a fence—me and another boy./ He's Chico./ He lives somewhere by us./ A boy pulled on our pants so when we got down we would fall./ So when I went to get down, well, he let go,/ and I jumped down and fell on Chico./ So the boy came around from the fence/ and he started to spit at us/ and we started to run where my daddy was./ But my daddy wasn't there./ He was in the front office,/ and so I told another man that works there./ And the boy went and got a coke and drank it and left./

SUBJECT BRADLEY:

Superman, I seen him last night . . . Clark Kent in Superman, do you know?/ An he, an he puts a aspirin, you know, a bad man put the aspirin in this little . . . in here,/ an, an he said, and this guy, well he told him . . . an he says how . . . an, an, an this guy pick-pocket him/ and he said, an the man said, "Is that the latest report?/ Let's see."/ An he said, "No."/ This man —see he's a bad man—and the guy he's working for—the boss— well, then he came up and he said, "Give the man some coffee./

Have some for me too."/ And then he went ahead with his money./

Although the first subject misses an opportunity to smooth his expression by subordinating his reference to Chico and location of Chico's home, his discourse is nevertheless relatively coherent. In organizing his material he subordinates four different elements, including one instance of second-order subordination. The second subject, Bradley, on the other hand, displays little or no plan of presentation for his account of the television program. His language is cluttered with false starts, and only once does he resort to subordination as an aid to organizing his material ("the guy he's working for"). Because he doesn't decide what to feature and what to subordinate, Bradley's talk lacks plan and order. In terms of language elements that can be identified and quantified, one major difference between Bradley and Manuel lies in the use of dependent clauses.

One difference in kinds of dependent clauses among three groups of subjects—low, high, and random subgroups—appears in Figure 6. Adverb and noun clauses are much more common than adjective clauses in the early years of school. In all of these, the high subgroup exceeds the low subgroup in incidence of use. Except for adjective clauses in grades two and three, the number of clauses increases each year. The adverb clause appears to discriminate between groups much more than does the noun clause.

One note of caution needs to be presented. Although the incidence of dependent clauses in expression is usually a measure of grammatical and semantic complexity, it is not an absolute measure of these matters. To be sure, LaBrant found an increasing proportion of dependent clauses a mark of increasing language development from grades four to nine, an increase that was a function both of mental and chronological age.[13] Her method, known as the subordination index, depends upon a count of all the dependent clauses in a transcript. The number of dependent clauses is then divided by the total number of clauses, both dependent and independent. This proves to be a helpful measure of increasing grammatical complexity, but it disregards other linguistic structures which also enable speakers and writers to compress their thought and to communicate their ideas ef-

---

[13]LaBrant, *op. cit.* (See p. 17.)

Figure 6

Incidence of Subordination: Frequency of Three Types
of Subordination for High, Random, and Low Subgroups of Subjects

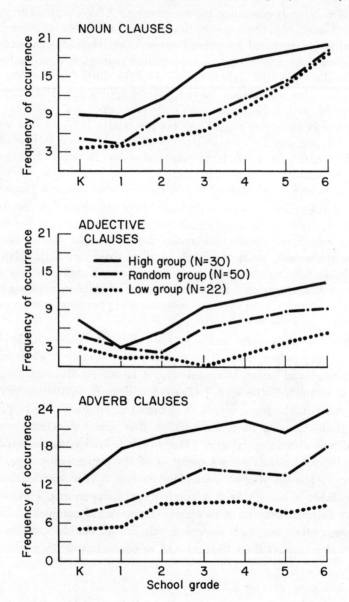

fectively. For instance, infinitives, participial phrases, gerunds, appositives, and other devices can contribute to compression and effectiveness.
Furthermore, complex sentences sometimes reflect confusion rather
than control; indeed some complex sentences could be improved by
being recast as simple sentences. Consequently, the reader must bear
in mind that indices of subordination, whether the straight count of
LaBrant or the weighted count used in this study, are not perfect in-
struments of analysis.

The present study employs two measures of grammatical complexity: (1) a weighted index of subordination granting heavier
weight to a dependent clause within another dependent clause or
modifying another dependent clause; and (2) a more highly refined
measure—the Chomsky technique of transformational grammar—which
identifies every means of grammatical complexity. These two methods
and their results are presented in the next few pages.

(1) The weighted index of subordination

For three subgroups—the high, low, and random—all dependent
clauses were tallied as follows:
   1 point for each dependent clause (first-order dependent clauses)
   2 points for any dependent clause modifying or within another
      dependent clause (second-order dependent clause)
   2 points for any dependent clause containing a verbal construc-
      tion such as an infinitive, gerund, or participle
   3 points for any dependent clause within or modifying another
      dependent clause which, in turn, is within or modifies another
      dependent clause (third-order dependent clauses)

As will be seen in Table 9, the high group uses such grammatical
complexity to a much greater extent than the other two groups. The
low group uses the least amount of grammatical complexity, although
all groups show an increase in grammatical complexity as chronological
age increases. In the data from which Table 9 is constructed, the boys
in the low group made scores consistently beneath those of the girls
in the low group. This was *not* true of the boys in the *high group* who
were superior to the girls in kindergarten as well as in grades one,
three, and five.

TABLE 9

Subordination Index
Incidence of Subordination Weighted According to
Use of Dependent Clauses and Verbal Phrases

Year in School	High Group N = 25		Random Group N = 25		Low Group N = 24	
	Median	Adjusted Median	Median	Adjusted Median	Median	Adjusted Median
K	19	.026	11	.019	6	.012
1	21	.027	15	.021	8	.013
2	30	.032	21	.023	9	.016
3	34	.028	23	.025	10.5	.021
4	42	.035	30	.027	13	.018
5	44	.036	32	.029	21	.024
6	53	.033	41	.030	24.5	.022

The median is the mid-score based on the weighted index.

The adjusted median is the mid-score of each subgroup when each subject's weighted index is divided by the total number of words in the subject's transcript. This adjusted score was computed in order to avoid favoring subjects who used more language than others.

(2) The technique of transformational grammar

For a more thorough study of grammatical complexity, this research has applied the methods of transformational grammar to the transcripts of two subjects. Transformational grammar identifies all forms of grammatical complexity, but it is a slow and long process of analysis. Its criteria are primarily structural. The combination of both structural and semantic criteria, used elsewhere in this study, is therefore set aside at this point and the present analysis limited to two structural questions: (1) How does the subject's grammar generate grammatical and ungrammatical utterances? and (2) By inference, what kind of grammatical model is the subject using in order to manipulate his structures?

In this research we have chosen samples from the speech of two children. The subjects were a boy (Dino) from the high group and a girl (Anngelina) from the low group. The three sets of utterances used for analysis here were collected from each of them during a six-year interval, at ages 8, 10, and 12.

Summary of Two Subjects' Transformational Skills at Age 10

DINO

Grammatical trans-		Frequency and types of
formations	19	grammatical transformations:
Faulty transformations*	4	Who or what	5
Total transformations:	23	Other questions	1
		Negatives	1
		Ellipses	6
		Conjunctions	4
		Indirect objects	1
		Comparatives	1
		Total	19

ANNGELINA

Grammatical trans-		Frequency and types of
formations	7	grammatical transformations:
Faulty transformations*	1	Who or what	2
Total transformations:	8	Negatives	2
		Indirect objects	1
		Conjunctions	2
		Total	7

*The faulty transformations were conjunction transformations.

This transformational analysis, although carried out for only two subjects, illustrates the possibilities of a more precise method of measuring grammatical complexity. Dino's ability to make grammatical sentences at the transformational level shows his greater control over structure than does Anngelina's persistence in creating all but seven of her sentences at the phrase structural level. Furthermore, Dino is not only producing more transformations than Anngelina but also more different kinds of transformations than Anngelina.

At the age of ten, Dino is handling grammatical transformation with a proficiency Anngelina has not yet reached even at the age of twelve. Examination of the transcripts for the low and high groups shows clearly that this difference prevails for all subjects in the two groups. The method, therefore, holds promise for future research.

Both the weighted index of subordination and the transformation analysis support the hypothesis that complexity of grammatical structure is associated not only with chronological age but also with proficiency in language. The high group uses more subordination than the low group and in particular uses more adverbial dependent clauses, second-order subordination, and subordination which includes infinitive and verbal phrases. Boys in the low group made consistently poorer scores in subordination than did girls in the low group.

Because the socioeconomic rank of the high group exceeds that of the low group, it appears that coherence through subordination is also related to socioeconomic status. The importance of socioeconomic status in relation to language appears not only on this matter of subordination but also on the measures of writing, mazes, subordinating connectives, reading, and conventional language. Bernstein, on the basis of research with British working class youth, found language proficiency grossly depressed in relation to scores on a nonverbal intelligence test.[14] He believes that the level of linguistic skill may be independent of potential intelligence and that different environments affect language structure. The linguistic differences he finds between working class youth do not, in his view, reflect differences in potential capacity. Rather they represent entirely different forms of the English language, forms which systematically orient children to differing relationships with people and the world about them. The middle class, for instance, uses forms of speech "in which the arrangement of syntax varies greatly from one individual to another and in which the formal possibilities of sentence organization are used to clarify meaning and make it more explicit." The lower working classes show "a rigidity of syntax, a limited and restricted use of the structural possibilities for sentence organization, a form of relatively condensed speech in which certain meanings are restricted and the possibility of their elaboration . . . reduced. . . ." Nothing in the present research with subjects on the West Coast of the United States controverts

---

[14]Basil Bernstein, "Language and Social Class," *British Journal of Sociology,* XI (1960), 271-276.

————, "Some Sociological Determinants of Perception," *British Journal of Sociology,* IX (1958), 159-174.

————, "Social Class and Linguistic Development: A Theory of Social Learning," *Education, Economy, and Society,* ed. A. H. Halsey, Jean Floud, and C. Arnold Anderson (New York: Macmillan [Free Press of Glencoe], 1961).

Bernstein's findings or conclusions. It also seems entirely possible that subjects from the least favored social economic categories can find themselves at a disadvantage in schools where the verbal linguistic skills of the middle class prevail. Such subjects may find themselves increasingly ill at ease and self-conscious to the point of avoiding oral performance. Such avoidance could, in turn, progressively affect performance in the related activities of reading and writing and in the present study could quite logically account for the larger number of mazes among the children in the low subgroup.

Coherence through the use of subordinating connectives

The accurate use of subordinating connectives such as *although, because,* and *unless* has been shown to develop with age. Watts devised a multiple-choice test with items such as the following:

He loves his mother, although

- a) she loves him.
- b) she is unkind to him.
- c) she is kind.
- d) he does not.[15]

Beginning in grade five, this Watts Test of Subordinating Connectives was administered, and the results are shown in Figure 7 for the high, low, and random groups. The socioeconomic status of the total group of subjects is again of interest. If the median scores and the range of scores are examined by socioeconomic level, we obtain the clear trends shown in Table 10. The highest and lowest socioeconomic groups overlap by only a few points, and the median of the highest group is almost double that of the lowest group. Notable also is the steady decrease in median as one reads down the socioeconomic scale. In conclusion, this sample shows an increasing use of subordinating connectors with chronological age, mental ability, and socioeconomic status.

Coherence through control of mazes

Too much difficulty with mazes—especially with long unresolved mazes—testifies not only to lack of fluency but also to poor control over speech and ineffectiveness in communicating with others. In Table 2 the reader has already noted that from kindergarten through

---

[15]Watts, *op. cit.*, pp. 82-84 and 302-305.

Figure 7

Ability to Use Subordinating Connectives
Median Scores of High, Random, and Low Groups
in Grades Five, Six, and Seven

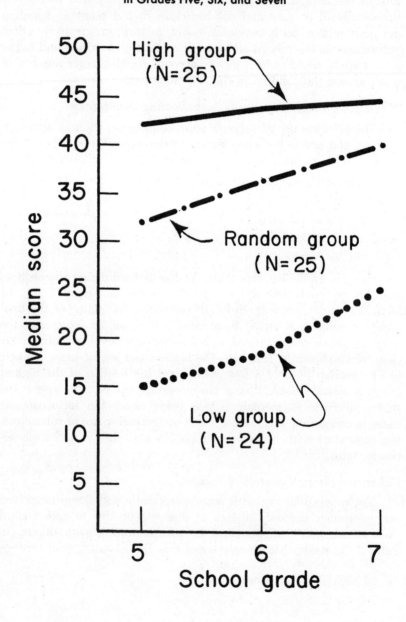

TABLE 10

Coherence through Subordinating Connectives
Relation between Achievement and Socioeconomic Level

Socioeconomic Level	Number	Median	Range
I	24	43	33-46
II	43	41	24-47
III	25	39	0-48
IV	30	34	4-46
V	46	33	0-48
VI	43	30	0-41
VII	21	24	3-36

grade three both low and high groups continue to have difficulties with mazes, the low group increasing the number of words per maze and the high group decreasing them slightly. From grade four through six, as has been previously noted, the volume of language needs to be taken into account. The high group consistently maintains a lower proportion of mazes and words in mazes than does the low group. On this matter, however, it is particularly important to note the measure of variability for all seven years. On words per maze the standard deviation is decreasing for the high group, but for the low group, this standard deviation is inconsistent and erratic.

Direct inspection of the mazes shows what is happening. Members of the high subgroup are controlling each maze, holding it down to a few words. For example, this maze from a boy in the high subgroup:

"That looks like a funny clown [holdin' a . .] holdin' a puppet in both hands."

On the other hand, members of the low subgroup are *increasing the number of words* in many of their mazes:

"[Then . then-n . you, then a boy hear you say . then-d] then they chase you."

"[These two are . . an this one who . who has .] these are *all* pirates having a party."

However, the low subgroup's inconsistent behavior in variability of words per maze may be a promising rather than a discouraging development, for it may well be a sign of growth through striving. They may also be striving in a situation where language is used in a manner they do not encounter in their homes. And in fact, data for grades four through six tend to bear out this hypothesis. (See Table 2.) Although the low group consistently performs more poorly than the high group in respect to mazes, words in mazes, and average words per maze, the subjects have succeeded in gaining better control over this obstacle to fluency. This is evidenced by the decline for the low group (grades four and five) in both incidence and variability of average words per maze. In grade six, a difference does occur, but it is not large.

For the present purpose the evidence on mazes does show that subjects are not in perfect control of their speech, whether they are rated low or high in language ability. It also shows that those highest in language ability speak somewhat more effectively and control more skillfully these difficulties of expression.

Coherence of spoken style

Among the features of spoken style which were classified, one category was coherent-to-incoherent. The high subgroup cannot be proved more coherent than the random group, but the low subgroup was less coherent than the random group. This latter difference was significant at the one percent level.

The evidence on spoken style also indicates that the subjects low in language ability follow more unconventional usage and speak less distinctly than the random group. They also tend to be slower in responding to conversation. Those high in language ability are more fluent, deliberate, conventional in their usage, and possibly more distinct in their speech than the total group.

SUMMARY ON EFFECTIVENESS AND CONTROL

Effectiveness and control of language have been examined by nine types of assessment. Although the subjects vary little in their use of the basic structural patterns of English, those high in language ability showed much greater dexterity in varying *the elements within these patterns*. Their repertoires for filling in the nominal positions and the movables of English syntax were clearly more varied than those of the group low in language ability. The high group also showed a greater sensitivity to the conventions of standard English, used provisional and conditional statements more often, showed greater competence in writing and reading, and excelled in coherence as measured by four different forms of assessment. The high group proves to be drawn from a higher socioeconomic status than the low group.

INTERRELATIONS AMONG THE LANGUAGE ARTS

The extent to which interrelations exist among the language arts is still a matter of speculation. Hildreth states that evidence of such relatedness exists, but her sources prove to be studies showing a positive relation between spelling and reading only.[16] Martin's study of the interrelations among language variables in the first grade produced contrary evidence. "There was little indication that the first grader who talked well would succeed in reading or that the poor speaker would have difficulty in it. Some children who were able to write well did poorly in both speaking and reading. Good readers were poor writers!"[17]

In this research interrelations have been charted for the following factors: oral language with written language; oral language with reading; reading with written language; and health with general language ability. The interrelations extend beyond the first grade and prove to be positive in the years beyond those covered in Martin's study.

In successive years of the present study, pupils at the third grade level who wrote well also ranked high in their use of oral language and in their reading. Table 11 arranges 188 third grade students in the study according to their ability to write. Those who are superior and above average on writing are also above average in speaking and reading. Those who are below average on any of the three measures are also below average on the other two.

Another interrelation already apparent at the third grade level is that those subjects who read well by the end of grade three are the subjects who have ranked high in oral language for the kindergarten and first three years of the study. As shown in Figure 8, not a single one of the twenty best readers in grade three is below the mean on oral language. For average and poor readers, however, this

---

[16] Gertrude H. Hildreth, "Interrelationships between Written Expression and the Other Language Arts," *Elementary English*, 31 (January, 1954), 40-43.

[17] Clyde Martin, "Developmental Interrelationships among Language Variables in Children of the First Grade," *Elementary English*, 32 (March, 1955), 167-71.

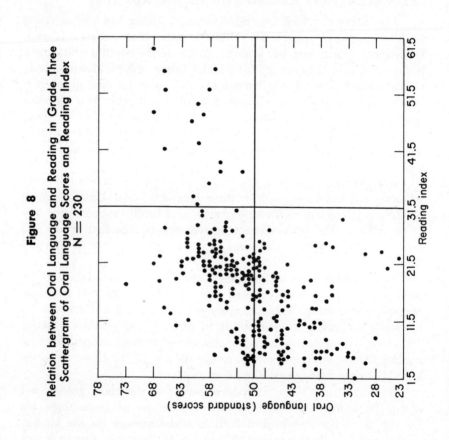

Figure 8

Relation between Oral Language and Reading in Grade Three
Scattergram of Oral Language Scores and Reading Index
N = 230

relationship with oral language is not apparent. This lack of relationship for average and poor readers could result from imprecision in the measure of reading achievement. The reading index in Figure 8 is based on teachers' records of the subjects' reading—mostly primers, basic readers, and supplementary readers at this early stage of learning reading. Teaching practice in the schools still tends to keep most students at the same reading tasks, and by grade three only the exceptional readers exhibit notable individual reading patterns. This may very likely be what Figure 8 reveals.

TABLE 11

Subjects Classified According to Writing Ability:
Average Scores on Reading and Speaking
Grade Three*

Written language: classification of subjects	Number in group	Reading achievement: average reading index of group	Oral language: average teachers' rating
I Superior group	19	25.8	3.73
II Above average group	42	23.0	3.77
III Below average group	88	18.5	3.27
IV Illiterate group	39	9.7	2.92
TOTAL GROUP	188	19.2	3.42

*The reader should note that data for grade three are not directly comparable to data for grade six which appear in Table 13. As indicated previously, the reading index for grade three was devised by the author whereas in grade six reading achievement ages (using the Stanford and California reading tests) were used.

As the subjects continue into the upper years of elementary school, a high interrelation between writing and reading becomes more apparent. Table 12 shows that fourth grade subjects in the lowest and highest quartiles in writing are comparably lower and higher in reading achievement. The data contained in this table are graphically presented in Figure 9.

TABLE 12

Relation between Reading and Writing
Percentage of Readers in Each Quartile Achieving
High, Average, and Low Writing Scores
Stanford Achievement Test

Average Reading Achievement Ages
(1956, Fourth Grade Tests)

Readers in Each Quartile	Writing Scores				N
	I	II	III	IV	$\bar{x}$RA
Q_1 f	0	5	16	19	40
% of Q_1	0.0	12.5	40.0	47.5	100.0
Q_2 f	6	16	15	3	40
% of Q_2	15.0	40.0	37.5	7.5	100.0
Q_3 f	10	19	6	4	39
% of Q_3	25.6	48.7	15.4	10.3	100.0
Q_4 f	17	12	7	3	39
% of Q_4	43.6	30.8	17.9	7.7	100.0
N_{ws}	33	52	44	29	158

		Reading Age in 1956, chronological age 9 to 9 years, 6 months		
		years-months		years-months
$\bar{x}$RA:	Q_1	6 - 4	to	8 - 3
	Q_2	8 - 4	to	9 - 4
	Q_3	9 - 5	to	10 - 5
	Q_4	10 - 6	to	13 - 3

$\bar{x}$RA = average reading achievement age on Stanford Achievement Test (average of paragraph and word meaning) (ages expressed in years and months)

ws = writing score

Q = quartile
Q_1 = lowest quartile
Q_2 = highest quartile

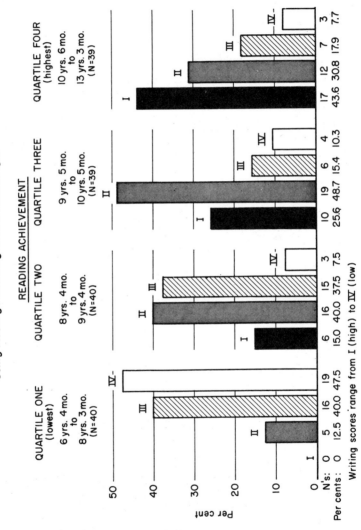

Figure 9

Relation between Reading and Writing
Using Average Reading Achievement Ages

TABLE 13

Interrelations among Reading, Writing, and Oral Language

Grade Six

Written language: classification of subjects	Number in group	Number reading above chronological age	Number reading below chronological age	Average reading achievement above or below expected age norm	Oral language: average teachers' ratings
I Superior group	21	21	0	+3 yr. and 6 mo.	4.08
II Good group	102	83	19	+1 yr. and 6 mo.	3.52
III Inferior group	73	20	53	−0 yr. and 9 mo.	3.01
IV Illiterate group	22	0	22	−2 yr. and 7 mo.	2.61
V Primitive group	4	0	4	−3 yr. and 6 mo.	2.53
TOTAL GROUP	222	124	98	+0 yr. and 5 mo.	3.15

From what has been presented to this point, there seem to be very definite interrelations in the language arts. And in fact, it will be seen that these interrelations become even more marked as we turn to later years of this study.

Table 13 classifies subjects in grade six according to their written language ability and presents the average reading achievement age and the average oral language rating (teachers' rating) for each classification. The superior group in writing has by far the highest reading achievement and the highest teachers' rating. Even more striking is the fact that *every* subject ranked superior in writing is *reading above* his chronological age; *every* subject ranked illiterate or primitive in writing is *reading below* his chronological age. The interrelation between reading and writing is presented graphically in Figure 10 for these same subjects, using medians and quartiles (Table 13 uses the arithmetic mean). As can be seen, on every statistical measure one fact is extremely clear in the present study: those who read well also write well; those who read poorly also write poorly.

In addition to the relation between reading and writing, data accumulated in this study show a high relation between reading and oral language. (See Figure 11.) The scattergram shown for grade six indicates a definite positive relation between these two elements of language with the pattern again being that a subject who excels in reading also excels in oral language. However, it does not so clearly follow that the poor reader will also be poor in oral language.

Although not quite as marked, there is also a positive relation between oral language and listening. (See Figure 12.) In this study a standardized listening test was first administered to subjects in the eighth grade. A more definite interrelation between listening and the other language arts may develop as subsequent listening tests are analyzed. Figure 12 shows that good listeners also excel in oral language. However, it does not follow that poor listeners will be poor in oral language skills.

Between health and language ability relations are positive, but it is difficult to determine a true measure of vitality. Health and energy, as rated somewhat crudely from the health records for each subject, show a low but positive relation with language ability (whether speaking, writing, or reading). Apathy, lassitude, and low vitality appear to be concomitants of low language ability for some subjects.

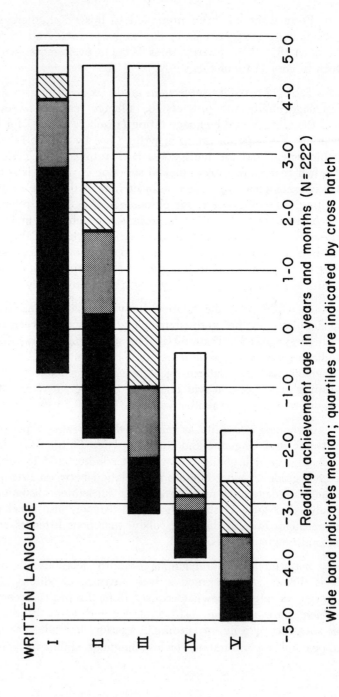

Figure 10

Relation between Reading and Writing in Grade Six

Written Language Scores Compared to Reading Achievement Above or Below Chronological Age

Reading achievement age in years and months (N=222)

Wide band indicates median; quartiles are indicated by cross hatch

WRITTEN LANGUAGE

I II III IV V

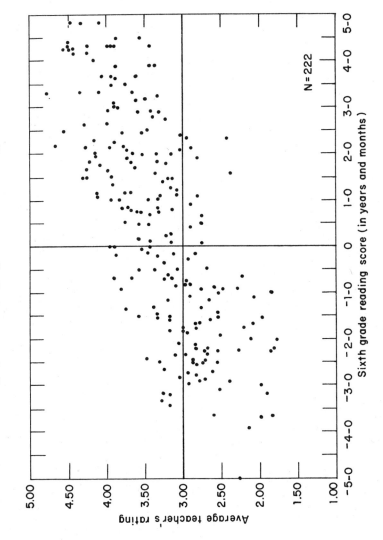

Figure 11

Relation between Oral Language and Reading in Grade Six
Scattergram of Oral Language Scores and Reading Scores

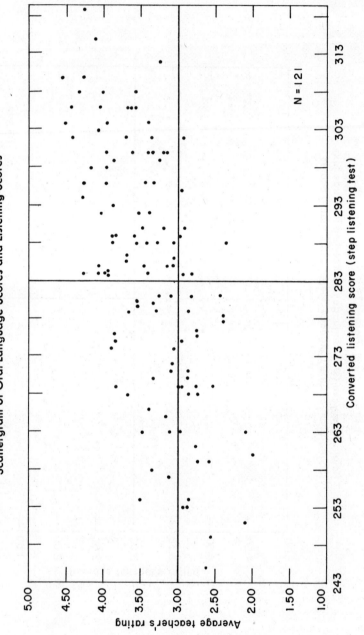

Figure 12

Relation between Oral Language and Listening in Grade Eight
Scattergram of Oral Language Scores and Listening Scores

This aspect of the study has been limited by available funds and the lack of an accurate or valid measure of vitality and energy. In the subsequent work of this longitudinal research, further efforts will be made to study these variables more intensely.

The highest correlation in this study, as could be expected, is between vocabulary and intelligence. Using the vocabulary test administered orally in the kindergarten and the Kuhlmann-Anderson group test of intelligence given in the second grade, we obtain a product-moment correlation of .844.

Chapter Three

CONCLUSIONS

This study has collected and analyzed language used by the same children through their kindergarten and first six years of elementary school. In the kindergarten year there were 338 subjects, and in grade six there are still 237 subjects remaining. One purpose of the research has been to develop methods of analysis which would make possible the scientific study of language in both its semantic and structural aspects. In this first phase of the study, the most important achievement has been the establishment of these objective methods for analysis. By combining the concept of a meaningful syntactic unit with phonological methods of segmentation, and by identifying and dealing with the noncommunicative elements, the *mazes,* a new and useful method of language analysis has been shaped. (See pages 4-14.) This method has proved to be a grid against which a wide range of important language phenomena can be silhouetted and measured. With the unit-and-maze grid, it becomes possible to quantify and relate to a solid base line such diverse and significant aspects of language as the following:

flexibility of sentence pattern and of elements within the sentence pattern

proportion of organization and rambling

variations from conventional usage, grammar, and syntax

degree of coherence through subordination

diversity and range of vocabulary

extent to which generalizations occur

freedom from language tangles or false starts (mazes)

amount of language and length of units of communication

number of separate concepts presented

amount of concreteness and abstractness

use of affective verbs and other emotional language

use of figurative language: metaphor, simile, irony, hyperbole, personification

These are only a few of the possible features to be analyzed by this method; their significance lies in the fact that they represent some of the elements certain to enter into any study of the development of language proficiency. Furthermore, the technique applies to oral or written language equally well, even though mazes are less likely to make an appearance in the written form.

By adding to the basic units of phonology and meaning the concept of the maze, a method has evolved which makes it possible to stabilize a phenomenon as nebulous and fluctuating as human symbolic language. No basis of measurement in language can—or should—ever be as absolute as meters or inches in the exact sciences. Nevertheless, the results of analyzing communication units and mazes are open to independent verification, permitting scientists working separately to reach the same conclusions. Checks on the method prove that two or more workers following the same set of coded directions get the same results within an exceptionally narrow range of minor differences.

SUMMARY OF FINDINGS

Fluency with Language

1. During the first seven years of schooling, the subjects speak more words in each succeeding year of measurement. They also increase the number of communication units and the average number of words spoken in each of those communication units. The high subgroup uses more words and units than does the low subgroup and maintains its initial superiority over those low in language ability (page 32). The fact that members of the high group use more communication units than do members of the low group is of particular significance because they are also, through greater subordination, reducing the number of units they need for expression. Even so, they produce *more* units than the low group.

2. During the first four years of schooling, the subjects as a whole decrease the number of mazes and words in mazes, but the average number of words in mazes increases for the low subgroup. Subjects rated as skillful in language are reducing both their incidence of mazes and the number of words per maze. In other words, the lower group says less than the high group and some of them have more difficulty in saying it (pages 32 and 33).

3. At the kindergarten level, subjects proficient in language have a median score of 67 on a vocabulary test of 100 items and the subjects low in language have a median score of 35 (page 37). Vocabulary and proficiency in language appear to be related.

4. Both the low and high groups of subjects use the same number of words from among the 12,000 most commonly used words in the English language; after that, the low group shows a higher incidence of words selected from the next 20,000 of the most commonly used words in the language (from 13,000 to 33,000). Thereafter, the high group gains ascendancy in the use of the least commonly used words of the English language (page 39 and Figure 3 on page 38).

5. As measured by spoken style of language, the high group is significantly more fluent than a random group selected from the total sample, but their readiness of response does not differ from the random sample. The low group is less fluent than the random group and there is evidence that they may be somewhat slower to respond in speech (page 42).

Effectiveness and Control

STRUCTURAL PATTERNS

1. The low group uses many more partial expressions—sentence patterns that are incomplete—than the high group. (See Tables 4a and 4b, pages 44-45.)

2. The group proficient in language employs the linking verb sentence pattern to a greater extent than does the low group. (See page 46).

3. The expletive type of sentence pattern is seldom used by the low group; for the high group, the use of it first increases, then decreases. The decrease in the use of the expletive type of sentence pattern could be due to stylistic development through instruction as well as reading. Teachers often discourage expletives because they preclude vivid and active expression.

4. The outer complement pattern is used only by the most able of the high group, and the inner complement pattern (indirect object) is seldom used by either group. For both patterns the incidence of use is slightly more frequent for the high group.

5. Except for the linking verb pattern and the use of partials, the differences in structural patterns used by the two groups are negligible. This similarity in use of patterns is considered to be an important finding of this study, especially when considered in relation to the findings which immediately follow.

ELEMENTS WITHIN THE STRUCTURAL PATTERNS

6. Although differences in structural patterns are not notable—with the exception of partials and linking verbs—very important differences do show up in the dexterity with which subjects use elements *within these structures.* The nominals, whether in subject or object position, and the movable elements show marked differences when low and high groups are compared. This holds true consistently for any syntactical nominal structure. It is assumed, from this, that predication, when it is studied, will also show similar marked differences. This finding on the elements of structural patterns is considered to be one of the important findings of this study and should be considered in relation to the findings (above) on the similarity of structural patterns. *Not pattern but what is done to achieve flexibility within the pattern* proves to be a measure of effectiveness and control of language at this level of language development.

7. In the movable elements of the patterns, the high group consistently shows a greater repertoire of clauses and multiples (movables within movables).

8. For subject nominals, the low group depends almost exclusively on nouns and pronouns. The high group can use noun clauses, infinitives, and verbals. (See pages 48-49.)

9. For nominals used as complements, both groups use nouns and pronouns with the same frequency, but the high group invariably exceeds the low group in the use of infinitives and clauses.

10. Boys in the low group are clearly more limited in their repertoire of syntax than girls in the low group. On the other hand, boys in the high group tend to excel the girls in the high group.

CONVENTIONAL USAGE AND GRAMMAR

11. Problems with use of verbs prove to be the most frequent kind of deviation from conventional usage in the elementary school.

12. Lack of agreement between subject and predicate, particularly in the third person singular, proves to be the major difficulty in

the use of verbs. Consistency of verb tense is another difficulty. The trends in this study show that the difficulty increases for Negro boys in grades one through three and decreases for Negro girls, provided that these Negro children came from homes using a southern Negro dialect.

13. For Negro subjects with southern background, using appropriately the verb *to be* proves to be twelve times as troublesome as for northern Caucasian or Negro subjects.

14. Subjects who are rated as most proficient in language are also those who manifest the most sensitivity to the conventions of language. The subject who, despite unconventional usage, exhibits verbal linguistic skill is the exception. (See page 52.)

TENTATIVE THINKING THROUGH THE USE OF PROVISIONAL AND CONDITIONAL STATEMENTS

15. Those subjects most proficient with language are the ones who most frequently use language to express tentativeness. Supposition, hypothesis, and conditional statements occur much less frequently in the spoken language of those lacking skill in language.

FIGURATIVE LANGUAGE AND GENERALIZATIONS

16. Very few examples of figurative language or of generalizations occur in the oral transcripts of the subjects' language.

READING AND WRITING

17. Those who are high in general language ability (the high group in this study) are also high in reading ability. Those who are low in general language ability (the low group in this study) are also low in reading ability. In addition, the gap between the high and the low groups is apparently widening from year to year. (See Figure 5, page 56.)

18. Writing ability is related to socioeconomic position. Those who were in the four lowest socioeconomic categories rated below average in writing and those who were in the highest three categories rated above average in writing.

COHERENCE THROUGH THE USE OF SUBORDINATION

19. Adverb and noun clauses are used by the total group much more frequently than adjective clauses.

20. The adverb clause discriminates between high and low groups better than do the noun and adjective clauses.

21. On an index of subordination, the high group uses this grammatical complexity to a greater extent than the random and low groups. Their precedence over the other two groups is consistent throughout all seven years of the study.

22. All three groups show an increasing use of subordination as chronological age increases.

23. The boys in the low group use consistently less subordination than the girls in the low group. On the other hand, the boys in the high group exceeded the girls in four out of the seven years of the study.

24. Transformational grammar, applied to two subjects, indicates that this kind of analysis is a valuable method of studying grammatical complexity. The girl from the low group was shown to be at least two years behind the boy from the high group in development of grammatical complexity.

25. Both the index of subordination and the transformational analysis show complexity of grammatical structure to be associated not only with chronological age but also with proficiency in language and with socioeconomic status. This is particularly interesting in relation to the theoretical explanation of this phenomenon published by the British linguist, Bernstein. (See Bibliography, page 91.)

COHERENCE THROUGH THE USE OF SUBORDINATING CONNECTIVES

26. The use of subordinating connectors increases with chronological age, mental ability, language ability, and socioeconomic status.

COHERENCE THROUGH CONTROL OF MAZES

27. From kindergarten through grade three, both low and high groups in language proficiency continue to have difficulties with language tangles, or mazes as they are called in this research. On number words per maze the standard deviation is decreasing for the high group and erratic for the low group. Apparently all of the high group members are gaining control of mazes, whereas the members of the low group are varying more in controlling these tangles. However, beginning with grade four the low group does show considerable improvement in controlling words per maze.

COHERENCE OF SPOKEN STYLE

28. The high group seems to be no more coherent in spoken style than a random group, whereas the low group is less coherent than the random group. The statistical evidence on this is not free from the possibility of error (some cells in the chi-square method contained fewer than six cases).

INTERRELATIONS AMONG THE LANGUAGE ARTS

29. In this study, reading, writing, listening, and speaking show a positive relation.

30. The subjects in the lowest and highest quartiles in writing are also lower and higher in reading achievement. Those who write well in grade three are also those who are above average in speaking and reading. Those who rate in the highest group in oral proficiency are also those who are completely above the median in reading for the random and low groups (also selected by a criterion of oral proficiency).

31. The highest correlation in the study is between vocabulary and intelligence as measured by the Kuhlmann-Anderson group test of intelligence. The product-moment correlation is .844. Vocabulary, success with group tests of intelligence, and proficiency with language constitute a cluster of traits (or, possibly, they are different manifestations of the same trait).

32. There is a low but positive relation between health and language proficiency. The measure of health used in this study is a crude measure, and the relation may well be higher.

A CONCLUDING STATEMENT

This research has achieved one of its major aims, the development of a fundamental method of analysis for studying children's language and for locating features of language meriting further study. How children vary in proficiency with language has also been charted in numerous ways, but clearly determined stages of development remain as yet unmarked. The data collected contain the evidence for such research as well as numerous other possibilities. As time permits, these possibilities will be pursued.

The most significant features to emerge from the work accomplished so far appear to be these:

. . . Not basic sentence pattern but what is done to achieve flexibility within pattern proves to be a measure of proficiency with language at this level. Since formal instruction in grammar—whether linguistic or traditional—seems to be an ineffective method of improving expression at this level of development, one can conclude that elementary pupils need many opportunities to grapple with their own thought in situations where they have someone to whom they wish to communicate successfully. Instruction can best aid the pupils' expression when individuals or small groups with similar problems are helped to see how *their own* expression can be improved. This instruction would take the form of identifying elements which strengthen or weaken communication, increase or lower precision of thought, clarify or blur meanings. For the pupils the approach would usually be through models, meaning, and reasoning rather than through the application of rules. On the other hand, the teacher would need to be aware of the structural problems behind the semantic difficulties and would be guided by research in determining what to emphasize or to ignore. Inductive reasoning toward generalizations would be more frequently encouraged than deductive applications to sentences not of the pupils' own creating. Occasionally the effectiveness or ineffectiveness of important ideas read or heard (e.g., recorded on tape) would be examined as a profitable reversal of self-expression through speaking and writing. Attention to structure at the expense of emphasizing successful communication could be a dangerous contribution of research not carefully interpreted.

. . . In this study the superiority of the high group in handling oral signals effectively—their skill at using pitch, stress, and pause— combined with their relative freedom from using partial structural patterns is impressive. It would be difficult not to conclude that instruction can yet do more than it has *with oral language.* Many pupils who lack skill in using speech will have difficulty in mastering written tradition. Competence in the spoken language appears to be a necessary base for competence in writing and reading. Modern equipment for recording and studying the spoken word makes possible marked advances in such instruction.

. . . Like the less proficient subjects' use of partial constructions, mazes used by all subjects in this study are impressive as a phenomenon of major significance. Their causes and a deeper study of their nature deserve a high priority in the next phase of the present research.

. . . The frequently recurring pattern of boys at the extreme ends of a number of measures is interesting. Whatever the causes, cultural or genetic, boys in this study do very poorly in language when they are low in language ability and excel when they are high in language ability.

. . . The persistently parallel variation of language proficiency and socioeconomic status should not be overlooked. It appears entirely possible that language proficiency may be culturally as well as individually determined. If children reared in families at the least favored socioeconomic positions receive a restricted language experience, if their early linguistic environment stresses only limited features of language potential, such children may indeed be at a disadvantage in school and in the world beyond school.

. . . The remarkable retention of subjects in this seven-year period of a longitudinal study (in a nation whose people are noted for moving about) is attributed to the persistence of the research staff and the fortunate fact that few families want to move away from the San Francisco Bay area. Even more remarkable has been the retention of subjects from the least favored socioeconomic groups. From the beginning it has been the policy of this research to avoid a sample skewed in the direction of upper class groups.

. . . Research studies of this kind are like preliminary explorations on a vast continent. The possibilities for greater knowledge of language behavior seem limitless.

BIBLIOGRAPHY

Bear, M. V. "Children's Growth in the Use of Written Language," *Elementary English Review*, 16 (1939), 312-319.

Bernstein, Basil. "Social Class and Linguistic Development: A Theory of Social Learning," *Education, Economy and Society, A Reader in the Sociology of Education*, ed. A. H. Halsey, Jean Floud, and C. Arnold Anderson. New York: Macmillan (Free Press of Glencoe), 1961, pp. 288-314.

Charters, W. W. "Minimum Essentials in Elementary Language and Grammar, A Second Report," *16th Yearbook of the National Society for the Study of Education*, Pt. I. Chicago: NSSE, 1917.

Chomsky, Noam. *Syntactic Structures*. 's-Gravenhage: Mouton and Co., 1957.

Chotlos, J. W. "Studies in Language Behavior: IV. A Statistical and Comparative Analysis of Individual Written Language Samples," *Psychological Monographs*, 56 (1944), 75-111.

Francis, W. Nelson. *The Structure of American English*. New York: Ronald Press, 1958.

Fries, C. C. *American English Grammar*. New York: Appleton-Century-Crofts, 1940.

Heider, F. K., and G. M. Heider. "A Comparison of Sentence Structure of Deaf and Hearing Children," *Psychological Monographs*, 52:1 (1940), 42-103.

Hildreth, Gertrude H. "Interrelationships between Written Expression and the Other Language Arts," *Elementary English*, 31 (1954), 40-43.

Hill, Archibald A. *Introduction to Linguistic Structures*. New York: Harcourt, Brace & World, 1958.

Johnson, Wendell. "Studies in Language Behavior: I. A Program of Research," *Psychological Monographs*, 56:2 (1944).

LaBrant, Lou. "A Study of Certain Language Developments of Children in Grades 4-12 Inclusive," *Genetic Psychology Monographs*, 14:4 (1933), 387-394.

Leonard, Sterling A. *Current English Usage*. English Monographs, No. 1. Champaign: National Council of Teachers of English, 1932.

Marckwardt, Albert H., and Fred G. Walcott. *Facts about Current English Usage*. New York: Appleton-Century-Crofts, 1938.

Martin, Clyde. "Developmental Interrelationships among Language Variables in Children of the First Grade," *Elementary English*, 32 (1955), 167-171.

Minnesota Scale for Paternal Occupations. Institute of Child Welfare, University of Minnesota. Minneapolis: University of Minnesota Press, n.d.

O'Rourke, L. J. *Rebuilding the English Curriculum: A Report of a Nationwide Study of English*. Washington: The Psychological Institute, 1934.

Piaget, Jean. *The Language and Thought of the Child*. New York: Harcourt, Brace, & World, 1926.

Pooley, Robert C. *Teaching English Usage.* New York: Appleton-Century-Crofts, 1946.

Rugg, H., L. Krueger, and A. Sondergaard. "Studies in Child Personality: I. A Study of the Language of Kindergarten Children," *Journal of Educational Psychology,* 20 (1929), 1-18.

Smith, M. E. "An Investigation of the Development of the Sentence and the Extent of Vocabulary in Young Children," *Child Welfare,* 3:5. Iowa City: University of Iowa, 1926.

Strickland, Ruth G. *The Language of Elementary School Children: Its Relationship to the Language of Reading Textbooks and the Quality of Reading of Selected Children.* Bulletin of the School of Education, Indiana University, 38:4 (July, 1962). Bloomington: Indiana University, 1962.

Thorndike, E. L., and I. Lorge. *The Teacher's Word Book of 30,000 Words.* New York: Teachers College, Columbia University, Bureau of Publications, 1944.

Watts, A. F. *The Language and Mental Development of Children.* Boston: D. C. Heath, 1948.

11-100